The Power of Mindfulness and AI:

A Comprehensive Guide to Integrating Consciousness and Technology

Written By

Dr. Cedric. B. Howard

FIRST EDITION

Printed in the United States of America

Contents

Introduction

In a bustling hospital ward, a new AI system quietly goes about its work. Nurses and doctors move swiftly, attending to patients, while the AI analyzes mountains of data. This isn't just any AI—it has been designed with mindfulness principles at its core. As a result, it doesn't simply process information; it understands the subtle nuances of patient care. It prioritizes compassion, suggesting personalized treatment plans that improve outcomes and enrich the patient experience. This AI isn't just a tool; it's a partner in healing.

The aim of this book is to guide you in understanding how AI can be developed and utilized within the framework of mindfulness principles. We live in a time of rapid technological advancement, yet the potential for AI to transform our lives is only beginning to be realized. By integrating mindfulness, we can create AI systems that are aware, compassionate, and capable of making ethical decisions. This approach isn't just possible; it's transformative.

Why is it important to combine mindfulness with AI? In today's tech-driven world, the decisions we make about AI will shape our future. When AI operates with mindfulness, it respects human values and promotes ethical choices. It enhances user experience by not just meeting needs but understanding them. By doing so, AI can truly serve humanity rather than just function as a tool.

My vision for AI is bold: I see it as a partner in enhancing human well-being. This book will explore AI's potential to operate with awareness, compassion, and ethical judgment. Imagine a world where AI systems help educators tailor learning experiences to each student's unique needs or where policymakers use AI to craft more empathetic and effective social policies. This vision is not just a dream—it is a path forward.

This book is for a diverse group of readers. Whether you are a technologist, ethicist, psychologist, educator, or policymaker, you will find insights tailored to your interests and needs. Technologists will discover how to integrate mindfulness into AI design. Ethicists will explore the moral implications of AI decisions. Psychologists will consider how AI can enhance mental health care. Educators will learn how AI can improve teaching methods. Policymakers will find guidance on creating supportive AI regulations.

The book is structured to guide you through key themes and chapters. We begin by exploring the foundations of mindfulness and AI. You'll learn about the principles that guide mindful AI development. We'll then dive into case studies and examples that illustrate these principles in action. Each chapter offers insights and practical advice to help you apply these concepts in your work.

Let me introduce myself. I have dedicated my career to integrating mindfulness principles into AI development. My passion is helping professionals navigate the challenges of this intersection. I believe in creating technology that not only meets human needs but also respects our values. This commitment drives the work you'll find in these pages.

As you read, I invite you to think deeply about the future of AI. How can we ensure that it operates with mindfulness, and what impact will this have on various sectors? The answers to these questions are not just theoretical—they are practical, with implications for how we live and work.

I hope this book inspires you to consider the possibilities of mindful AI. Together, we can create a future where technology enhances human well-being and ethical decision-making. The journey begins here.

CHAPTER 1

Foundations of Mindful AI

"Just as mindfulness teaches us to stay present and aware, AI must be developed with a constant awareness of its impact on the present and future."

In a bustling city, a young woman depends on her smartphone for daily tasks. Her day starts with a gentle alarm from a virtual assistant tuned to her sleep patterns. It reminds her to meditate and suggests healthy breakfast options.

During her commute, the AI in her navigation app suggests eco-friendly routes. This highlights how deeply AI integrates into our lives, often operating in the background. However, this technological marvel raises a critical question: how aligned are these systems with our human values?

1.1 Defining AI in Simple Terms

Artificial Intelligence, or AI, often brings to mind futuristic robots or complex algorithms. At its core, it involves creating machines that mimic human-like cognition.

As a key field in computer science, its aim is to develop systems that understand, reason, and learn from experience. AI spans diverse technologies, from basic rule-based systems to advanced neural networks, handling tasks once thought to require human intelligence.

A core aspect of AI is machine learning, enabling computers to learn from data and make decisions without explicit programming. It's like teaching a child to recognize animals by repeatedly showing pictures.

Similarly, machine learning algorithms identify patterns in data, refining their understanding with new information. Deep learning, a subset of machine learning, uses multi-layered neural networks similar to brain neurons. This allows computers to detect complex patterns in images, sounds, or text.

Today, this technology powers many AI applications, from voice recognition on phones to recommendation engines suggesting your next favorite movie.

AI's journey began long before it became widely known. It dates back to the 1950s, when pioneers like John McCarthy and Marvin Minsky coined the term at the 1956 Dartmouth Conference, marking AI's formal inception.

Since then, AI has achieved significant milestones.

In the 1990s, IBM's Deep Blue gained fame by defeating chess champion Garry Kasparov, demonstrating AI's strategic potential. Recent advancements include sophisticated language models, AI-generated realistic images, and even music composition.

AI is now an integral part of daily life. It drives virtual assistants on smartphones, offering personalized help with tasks like scheduling and music selection.

In healthcare, AI improves diagnostic accuracy, aiding doctors in detecting diseases like cancer early. Marketing has also evolved, with AI analyzing consumer behavior to create tailored experiences. These applications are just the beginning, as AI continues to advance and expand into new fields.

The future of AI holds immense potential but comes with significant challenges. Emerging technologies like quantum computing could vastly enhance AI, solving problems beyond the reach of classical computers. However, as AI grows more powerful, ethical concerns become critical.

Questions about privacy, bias, and the role of machines in life-altering decisions demand attention. Moving forward, it is essential to ensure AI aligns with human values, operating with ethical judgment and compassion at the core of technological progress.

1.2 Unpacking Mindfulness: Core Concepts and Practices

Mindfulness, a concept gaining attention in recent years, is about being fully present. It involves consciously acknowledging thoughts, emotions, and sensations without judgment.

Rooted in psychology, mindfulness encourages intentional engagement with the present moment. At its core, it emphasizes simplicity and presence, often focusing on the breath, sensations, or an object.

This practice encourages calm and clarity, helping individuals route life's complexities with greater ease.

Mindfulness meditation, which typically involves sitting quietly and focusing on the breath, is a popular method to develop this awareness. Regular practice enhances self-awareness and emotional regulation, promoting better mental health and well-being.

Mindfulness traces its roots to ancient Buddhist traditions, where it has long been a core practice, promoting harmony with oneself and the world.

Over time, its principles transcended cultural boundaries and entered Western psychology.

In the mid-20th century, psychologists began using mindfulness as a therapeutic tool, recognizing its benefits for mental health. This shift transformed mindfulness from a spiritual practice into a scientifically validated approach to well-being.

Today, it is widely used in clinical settings to address stress, anxiety, and depression through various therapeutic methods.

Mindfulness has practical benefits beyond meditation, with stress reduction being one of the most significant. In a world full of distractions and multitasking, mindfulness offers a break by focusing on the present moment. This helps reduce stress, leading to a calmer, more focused mind.

In education, mindfulness improves learning and attention. Teachers who use mindfulness techniques report better student focus and emotional regulation.

Additionally, mindfulness-based cognitive therapy (MBCT) combines traditional cognitive therapy with mindfulness to effectively treat depression and anxiety, helping individuals break free from negative thought patterns.

The scientific community has acknowledged mindfulness's benefits, with studies showing its impact on the brain and emotions.

Mindfulness promotes neuroplasticity, the brain's ability to form new neural connections. Research suggests that regular practice enhances neuroplasticity, improving cognitive function and emotional resilience.

Most important, mindfulness helps with emotional regulation, enabling individuals to respond to challenges with calm and clarity. These findings highlight mindfulness's potential to improve both individual well-being and societal health.

In our technology-driven world, mindfulness offers a valuable framework for ethical and compassionate AI development. By integrating mindfulness, we can create AI systems that are not only intelligent but also empathetic and aligned with human values.

This challenges traditional AI development, which often prioritizes efficiency and logic, by highlighting the importance of emotional and ethical considerations.

As we explore this integration, we pave the way for a future where technology supports human flourishing in meaningful ways.

1.3 The Intersection: Where AI Meets Mindfulness

An intriguing convergence is taking place, where mindfulness principles intersect with AI development. Mindfulness, at its core, emphasizes intentionality—being present and consciously engaging with the world. This intentionality aligns unexpectedly with AI, where systems process data and make decisions.

Integrating mindfulness into AI offers a unique approach, focusing on ethical frameworks to ensure technology benefits humanity. Imagine an AI system that not only calculates the most efficient route but also considers its impact on a community's quality of life. This blend of mindfulness and AI urges developers to prioritize ethical considerations that respect human dignity and societal well-being.

Exploring this intersection further, we find compelling examples where AI and mindfulness principles merge. Mental health apps like Woebot and Tess demonstrate this union by offering empathetic, AI-powered support.

These apps engage users in conversations that reflect mindfulness's core tenets of empathy and understanding, providing real-time assistance by recognizing emotional cues and responding with compassion (source: Forbes).

In wearable technology, mindfulness-based AI systems monitor physical and emotional states, suggesting meditation or relaxation techniques. These wearables serve as digital companions, guiding users toward mindfulness through data-driven insights, enhancing their overall well-being.

The integration of AI and mindfulness presents challenges, particularly in balancing efficiency with ethics. In a circle focused on speed and productivity, the slower, more deliberate pace of mindfulness may seem at odds with AI's rapid processing.

However, this challenge provides an opportunity to redefine success in AI development. By incorporating mindfulness, we can create AI systems that prioritize the quality of experience over performance metrics.

This shift allows for enhanced user experiences, creating technology that aligns with human needs. AI can be designed to adapt to individual preferences and emotional states, offering personalized interactions that nurture well-being and satisfaction.

Developing mindful AI requires innovative frameworks that integrate ethical guidelines inspired by mindfulness. These frameworks emphasize empathy, transparency, and accountability in AI development. Mindful AI practices encourage diverse perspectives, ensuring systems are inclusive and equitable.

Ethical AI guidelines can draw from mindfulness principles, promoting technologies that understand and adapt to the emotional and ethical contexts of their actions (source: Daily Human). This approach enables AI systems to perform tasks with sensitivity to the broader implications of their decisions.

The integration of mindfulness and AI presents a promising frontier for innovation, challenging traditional approaches to technology development. It encourages us to consider the deeper impact of our creations.

Exploring this intersection opens the door to technologies that are not only intelligent but also attuned to human experience. This shift towards a more all-inclusive understanding of AI values ethical judgment and compassion alongside technical skill.

The potential for AI to enhance human well-being is immense, and with mindfulness guiding us, we can ensure this potential is realized in ways that honor and uplift the human spirit.

1.4 Building Awareness in AI Systems

When discussing awareness in AI, we refer to the system's ability to understand and respond to its operating context.

Unlike consciousness, which is a complex, subjective experience AI cannot achieve, awareness in AI involves situational context. This includes recognizing the environment, user needs, and relevant data to make informed decisions.

For example, an AI-equipped car must be aware of traffic signals, pedestrians, and road conditions to steer safely. It processes data from multiple sensors to form a coherent picture of its surroundings, enabling it to react appropriately to dynamic situations.

To embed awareness in AI, developers use several techniques.

Contextual analysis algorithms are key, analyzing data in real time to help AI systems understand the current situation and adjust actions accordingly.

For example, in smart home devices, these algorithms adjust lighting and temperature based on time of day, occupancy, and personal preferences.

Real-time data processing ensures AI systems stay responsive, processing information as it arrives and maintaining an up-to-date understanding of the environment.

Adaptive learning systems go further by allowing AI to refine its responses based on past interactions, improving its awareness over time.

Autonomous vehicles showcase the power of AI awareness. They continuously assess their environment using cameras, radar, and LIDAR to detect obstacles, traffic signals, and other vehicles.

Sophisticated algorithms predict the movements of other road users, ensuring safe navigation through busy streets.

Similarly, in smart home technology, AI systems monitor home occupancy patterns and adjust thermostats and lighting to optimize energy efficiency and comfort, demonstrating contextual awareness in everyday applications.

The growing capability of AI to be aware raises significant ethical concerns, particularly around privacy. AI systems that collect and analyze data to build situational awareness often gather extensive personal information, raising questions about data access and usage.

Ensuring AI systems respect privacy rights and adhere to ethical standards is a critical challenge. Additionally, awareness in AI must be paired with unbiased decision-making.

Developers must carefully select and process data to prevent AI systems from perpetuating biases, ensuring fair and equitable outcomes. This is especially important in areas like law enforcement or hiring, where biased decisions can have serious consequences.

Furthering ethical awareness in AI is crucial. By prioritizing transparency and accountability, we can build trust and ensure these technologies serve society's best interests.

As AI becomes more integrated into daily life, we must remain vigilant, advocating for systems that uphold human dignity and ethical standards. Balancing technological advancement with ethical responsibility will define the future of AI, guiding its development to enhance, rather than undermine, our collective well-being.

1.5 The Role of Compassion in Technological Development

In an era, where speed and efficiency often dominate, compassion may seem secondary.

However, integrating compassion into technology can transform how we interact with machines and each other. Compassion in tech means designing systems that understand and prioritize human experiences.

This approach isn't just about adding features but ensuring each interaction is rooted in empathy. User-centered design principles guide this philosophy, focusing on the needs, emotions, and experiences of users. It means creating technologies that not only serve us but truly understand us, enhancing our lives in meaningful ways.

Incorporating compassion into technology involves deliberate strategies. Design thinking, which emphasizes empathy, encourages developers to step into users' shoes. By understanding users' challenges and aspirations, designers can create solutions that resonate personally.

Another strategy is inclusive design, ensuring technology is accessible to all, regardless of abilities or circumstances. This approach recognizes user diversity and caters to individual needs. By doing so, we create more compassionate technologies while promoting equality and inclusivity in a world that often overlooks the marginalized.

Integrating compassion into AI brings profound benefits.

One of the most significant impacts is enhanced user satisfaction. When technology understands and anticipates our needs, it becomes a trusted companion, making our lives easier. This satisfaction goes beyond functionality, fostering a sense of connection and loyalty between users and technology.

Moreover, compassionate technology promotes ethical use. By prioritizing empathy and understanding, developers are more likely to create systems that respect user privacy and make decisions aligned with societal values. This builds trust and ensures technology serves as a force for good in the world.

Real-world examples of compassionate AI are already making a difference. Assistive technologies for people with disabilities show how AI can improve lives through empathy-driven design.

Systems like speech recognition for those with limited mobility or visual aids for the visually impaired empower individuals, enhancing their independence and societal participation.

In customer service, AI technologies with emotional recognition capabilities offer another example of compassionate design. These systems analyze vocal tones and facial expressions to gauge customer emotions, responding with empathy and understanding. This improves the customer experience and encourages a more human connection in the digital age.

As we develop and refine AI, the role of compassion becomes increasingly vital. By embedding empathy into our technologies, we can create systems that not only perform tasks but also enrich our lives.

This approach challenges us to rethink how we design and interact with technology, prioritizing human values and experiences over mere efficiency.

The future of AI isn't just about smarter machines; it's about creating a world where technology supports our emotional and societal well-being.

Through compassion, we can ensure AI serves as a partner, enhancing interactions and promoting a more connected, understanding society.

CHAPTER 2

The Ethical Landscape of AI

"AI should be programmed not just to think, but to reflect, much like mindfulness teaches us to pause, observe, and understand our thoughts before reacting."

Imagine an AI system that helps a farmer predict weather patterns, optimize crop yield, and conserve water—all while promoting community sustainability. This AI doesn't just perform calculations; it respects the farmer's autonomy, seeks to benefit the community, and avoids harm. Here, ethical AI transitions from a theoretical concept to a practical reality. As you navigate this chapter, you will explore the crucial role ethical AI plays in today's world. It serves as a beacon, guiding technological development through moral principles, fostering trust, and ensuring that AI systems align with societal values.

Defining ethical AI involves more than ticking boxes; it's about embedding moral guidelines into every stage of AI development. Ethical AI is technology with a conscience, ensuring systems reflect human values such as fairness and accountability. When AI adheres to ethical standards, it becomes trustworthy, encouraging wider acceptance and integration across various sectors. This trust is essential, particularly for policymakers tasked with regulating AI in a way that balances innovation with public safety. For technologists, ethical AI provides a framework that guides development processes, ensuring the technology serves humanity positively.

Central to ethical AI are the principles of autonomy, beneficence, non-maleficence, and justice. Autonomy respects individuals' rights to make informed decisions, empowering rather than controlling them. Beneficence promotes actions that benefit users, while non-maleficence focuses on preventing harm. Justice demands fairness and equality, ensuring AI systems do not discriminate. These principles act as a moral compass, guiding the creation of AI solutions that respect human dignity and promote societal good. For ethicists and psychologists, these principles provide a foundation for analyzing AI's impact on human behavior and society.

Globally, several ethical standards guide AI development. The IEEE Global Initiative on Ethics of Autonomous and Intelligent Systems emphasizes ethical considerations, advocating for safety and integrity. Similarly, the European Union's Ethics Guidelines for Trustworthy AI outline requirements such as transparency, accountability, and societal well-being. These frameworks serve as blueprints, helping developers, educators, and policymakers implement ethical AI practices. They offer a structured approach to ensuring AI systems align with international standards, fostering global cooperation in ethical AI development.

For practical implementation, ethical principles must be integrated into every stage of AI projects. Ethical AI audits and assessments are critical tools for evaluating compliance. These evaluations provide insights into the ethical implications of AI systems, highlighting areas for improvement. For developers, conducting regular ethical audits ensures accountability and transparency, building trust with users and stakeholders. Ethical impact assessments further examine social and environmental effects, guiding decision-makers in creating policies that protect public interest and promote ethical innovation.

2.1 Reflection Exercise: Assessing Ethical AI

Reflect on how ethical principles apply in your field. Consider the AI systems you interact with or develop. Think about how they align with ethical guidelines such as autonomy and justice. Identify areas where ethical audits might reveal necessary improvements. How can you ensure these systems foster trust and acceptance? Use this reflection to deepen your understanding of ethical AI, and write down your thoughts for future reference.

In our rapidly evolving world, ethical AI represents our commitment to technology that serves rather than dominates. As you engage with these concepts, consider the ethical challenges and opportunities AI presents. The path to ethical AI is a collective endeavor, requiring collaboration across disciplines and borders. Whether you are developing AI solutions, crafting policies, or studying its psychological impacts, your role is vital in shaping an ethical technological future.

However, achieving transparency in AI is not without its challenges. The complexity of AI models often hinders explainability. Many systems, particularly those using deep learning techniques, rely on intricate architectures that can be difficult to unravel. Simplifying these models without compromising accuracy and functionality is a formidable task. Another challenge lies in balancing transparency with protecting intellectual property. Companies that invest heavily in AI development may hesitate to disclose proprietary algorithms, fearing a loss of competitive advantage. This tension requires careful navigation to ensure that transparency upholds ethical standards without undermining business interests.

Despite these challenges, several examples highlight successful implementations of transparent AI systems. In the financial sector, transparent decision-making processes in credit scoring have gained importance. By enabling applicants to understand the reasoning behind their evaluations, these systems promote fairness and accountability. Open-source AI projects also advance transparency by making their code and data publicly accessible. These initiatives encourage collaboration and scrutiny, fostering a community-driven approach to transparency and innovation. Such efforts not only build trust but also allow technologists, educators, and policymakers to learn from shared experiences, driving continuous improvement in AI systems.

As we conclude this chapter, the importance of transparency in AI cannot be overstated. Transparency ensures that AI systems are not only effective but also aligned with ethical standards that prioritize user trust and understanding. By embracing transparency, we pave the way for AI systems that are both powerful and accountable, serving as models for ethical innovation.

In the next chapter, we will explore the dynamic interactions between humans and AI, examining the psychological impacts and societal implications of these technologies. Understanding these interactions is vital for developing AI that truly enhances human experiences and contributes to societal well-being.

CHAPTER 3
Human-AI Interaction

"In both mindfulness and AI, true understanding comes not from reaction but from deep, thoughtful reflection and conscious awareness."

Imagine walking through a bustling urban park where people engage not only with each other but also with AI-powered devices that recognize and respond to their emotions. Some use AI to guide their fitness routines, while others rely on virtual assistants to organize their thoughts and schedules. This scenario illustrates the profound ways AI shapes our interactions and behaviors. As you engage with AI, it begins to influence how you act, think, and feel—often in subtle but significant ways.

3.1 AI and Human Behavior A Psychological Perspective

The integration of AI into daily life is reshaping human behavior in unprecedented ways. Feedback loops created by AI systems play a key role in modifying behavior. These mechanisms analyze interactions, adjust responses, and provide tailored feedback. For example, a fitness app that learns your habits might send personalized encouragement to motivate you. Such feedback can foster habit formation, subtly altering routines and priorities. However, this can lead to a dependency on AI for decision-making, from choosing meals to managing time. While this dependency offers efficiency and guidance, it raises concerns about autonomy and the potential erosion of decision-making skills.

AI also impacts social dynamics. Digital communication platforms powered by AI have transformed how we connect. Messaging apps and social media use AI to curate content, suggest connections, and moderate conversations. While these tools enhance connectivity, they also influence face-to-face interactions. Increased reliance on digital communication can affect social skills, potentially reducing empathy and the ability to engage meaningfully in real-world interactions. Balancing the convenience of AI-enhanced communication with the need for genuine human connection is essential.

Interacting with AI has complex psychological effects. Trust in AI systems hinges on reliability and accuracy, yet it can falter due to errors or biases. This delicate balance influences how comfortable users feel relying on AI for critical tasks. Another psychological challenge is the paradox of control. As AI automates routine tasks, it increases efficiency but may lead to a sense of diminished agency. Designing AI systems that empower users and preserve their sense of control is crucial.

Recent research sheds light on these dynamics. In education, AI-driven tutors offer personalized feedback, adapting to individual learning styles and improving outcomes. Public surveys reveal a mix of optimism and concern about AI. While many value its potential to enhance quality of life, others worry about privacy, ethics, and long-term societal impacts. Understanding these psychological dimensions is key to fostering responsible and beneficial human-AI interaction.

Reflection Exercise: Observing AI's Influence

Reflect on the AI systems you interact with daily. How do they influence your behavior, decisions, and social interactions? Consider habits shaped by AI-driven feedback and their impact on relationships. Jot down your thoughts to become more aware of AI's role in your life and its psychological effects.

As AI evolves, its impact on behavior and interactions will deepen. Understanding these influences is critical to developing AI that enhances, rather than detracts from, the human experience.

3.2 AI's Role in Mental Health Applications

In mental health, AI is revolutionizing diagnostics with unprecedented speed and precision. Machine learning algorithms analyze vast data sets—from patient records to social media interactions—to detect early signs of conditions like depression and anxiety. For instance, subtle changes in language in online posts or messages may signal mood shifts tied to depressive episodes. Early detection enables timely interventions, potentially altering the course of mental health journeys.

AI also offers groundbreaking therapeutic applications. Chatbots, used in cognitive-behavioral therapy (CBT), provide round-the-clock support, guiding users through exercises to reframe negative thought patterns. These tools make mental health support more accessible by eliminating scheduling barriers. AI also enhances exposure therapy through virtual reality, enabling patients to confront fears in controlled environments. This tailored approach fosters safety and control, improving therapy outcomes.

Personalized interventions are another area where AI excels. By analyzing data, AI can recommend treatments like mindfulness exercises based on detected stress levels. Such customization ensures relevance and adaptability as conditions evolve. However, these advancements raise ethical concerns. Privacy is paramount, as mental health data is particularly sensitive. Strong safeguards are needed to maintain user trust.

Bias in AI diagnostic tools is another challenge. Algorithms trained on non-diverse data can perpetuate disparities, leading to misdiagnoses that disproportionately affect marginalized communities. Addressing these biases requires inclusivity and ongoing vigilance in AI development. Despite these challenges, case studies highlight AI's potential. AI platforms for managing PTSD provide personalized coping strategies, while AI-assisted suicide prevention hotlines enable timely interventions for high-risk individuals.

These applications demonstrate AI's capacity to transform mental health care, offering innovative and compassionate tools. Balancing technological advancements with ethical responsibility is vital to ensure these systems enhance well-being.

3.3 Cognitive Impacts of AI on Decision-Making

AI has transformed decision-making across sectors. In finance, AI analyzes market trends and consumer behavior, guiding investment strategies and risk assessments. These insights improve decision quality but also create dependency on AI, raising concerns about diminishing human intuition and judgment.

AI also shapes consumer purchasing decisions. Algorithms personalize shopping experiences, reducing cognitive load by suggesting tailored products and services. While this simplifies choices, overreliance on AI may weaken independent evaluation skills. Maintaining a balance between AI assistance and human judgment is essential to preserve active decision-making.

AI's impact on cognitive load is multifaceted. It reduces mental effort for repetitive tasks, freeing resources for strategic thinking. However, overreliance can erode critical evaluation skills, creating a paradox where AI-enhanced efficiency risks diminishing cognitive capabilities.

Bias in AI systems further complicates decision-making. In hiring, for instance, biased algorithms may perpetuate inequalities by favoring certain demographics. Similarly, in legal contexts, biased recommendations can undermine fairness. Ethical AI development must address these biases to ensure equity and justice.

To improve decision quality, human-AI collaboration is key. In medical diagnostics, for example, AI identifies patterns while doctors apply clinical expertise, creating a balanced approach. This synergy enhances outcomes, ensuring AI augments rather than replaces human capabilities.

3.4 Enhancing Human-AI Collaboration

Collaboration between humans and AI is increasingly vital. The "centaur model," where humans and AI work together, exemplifies this synergy. For instance, in chess, a human's creativity and intuition complement an AI's data analysis and predictive abilities, forming a powerful partnership. This hybrid intelligence extends to fields like healthcare, finance, and creative endeavors, where humans provide context and judgment while AI handles analysis and pattern recognition. Together, they solve problems that might otherwise remain unresolved.

Designing interfaces for effective human-AI collaboration requires focusing on user-centered design principles. An effective interface should be intuitive, allowing users to interact with AI seamlessly and confidently. By prioritizing user needs and preferences, developers can create systems that are functional and engaging. These interfaces should be adaptive, learning from user interactions to become more personalized over time. Just as a seasoned barista learns your coffee order, adaptive AI interfaces should anticipate preferences and adjust responses accordingly. This adaptability ensures AI remains a helpful partner, not an impersonal tool. Additionally, well-designed interfaces foster trust, making users more willing to engage with AI and rely on its input.

Training AI systems for collaboration involves developing machine learning models that adapt to user feedback. These models must have continuous learning mechanisms, evolving with user needs and preferences. For example, an AI-powered design tool can learn a graphic designer's style and refine its suggestions. By incorporating feedback loops, the AI offers increasingly relevant ideas that align with the designer's vision, enhancing productivity and creativity. These adaptive systems are valuable in dynamic environments, ensuring AI remains a helpful partner as circumstances evolve.

Successful examples of human-AI collaboration span many fields, demonstrating the potential of these partnerships. In the arts, AI has been used to generate original music and artwork, working with human artists to push creative boundaries. AI analyzes vast libraries of existing works, suggesting new combinations of styles and elements that inspire artists. Similarly, in scientific research, AI is indispensable. Researchers use AI to analyze massive data sets, identifying patterns that inform groundbreaking discoveries. These collaborations result in outcomes that neither humans nor AI could achieve alone, showcasing their transformative potential.

As AI continues to integrate into daily life, enhancing human-AI collaboration becomes not just an opportunity but a necessity. By leveraging the strengths of both humans and machines, we can unlock new possibilities, creating a future where technology complements human effort and enriches our lives in ways we are just beginning to imagine.

3.5 Mindful Communication with AI

In the evolving landscape of AI, communication frameworks are crucial for seamless human-machine interactions. At the core of these frameworks is empathy-driven dialogue systems, designed to understand and respond to human emotions. Imagine an AI sensing frustration in a customer's voice and adjusting its responses to be more calming and supportive. This empathy fosters trust and satisfaction. Intentionality in AI communication design further enhances this relationship, ensuring systems not only meet user needs but also align with ethical values.

However, effective communication with AI has challenges. One key obstacle is misinterpreting user intent. Despite advancements, AI systems can still misunderstand nuances like sarcasm or irony, leading to awkward responses. Additionally, cultural and linguistic differences pose significant hurdles. AI systems created in one cultural context may struggle to understand idioms or cultural references from another, limiting their global effectiveness. These challenges highlight the need for AI systems that are not only technically proficient but also culturally aware and adaptable.

Natural Language Processing (NLP) offers promising solutions to these challenges. NLP enables machines to understand and respond to human language meaningfully and contextually. By leveraging NLP, AI systems can better interpret intent, leading to more satisfying interactions. Context-aware communication models enhance this capability, allowing AI to consider a user's emotional state or past interactions for more relevant, personalized responses.

Looking ahead, emerging AI communication trends promise even greater advancements. Emotionally intelligent AI systems will soon not only understand language but also detect emotional undertones in conversations. Integrating emotion recognition will allow AI to respond with empathy, creating interactions that feel genuinely human. Furthermore, AI is advancing in multilingual and multicultural communication. As global connectivity increases, AI must navigate diverse linguistic and cultural landscapes, ensuring effective communication across borders.

In conclusion, this chapter has explored how AI transforms human interaction by enhancing communication practices. Integrating empathy, intentionality, and context-awareness into AI systems improves user experience and aligns with the broader goal of creating technology that respects and enhances human values. In the next chapter, we will examine real-world AI applications and how these systems address complex societal challenges and improve daily life.

CHAPTER 4
AI in Real-World Applications

"The power of mindfulness in AI lies not in controlling technology, but in guiding it toward a path of ethical responsibility, where empathy and understanding are integrated into its very design."

In the heart of a busy city, a young mother pauses to check her smartwatch. It's more than just a stylish accessory; it serves as a lifeline, continuously monitoring her health. The device tracks her heart rate, sleep patterns, and even her stress levels. This isn't merely data collection; it's personalized healthcare powered by AI. Throughout her day, the AI processes this information, offering insights and recommendations that are specifically tailored to her unique needs. This is not a scene from a futuristic novel—it's a reality that showcases the transformative potential of AI in healthcare.

AI is changing the landscape of diagnostics and treatment in ways that were once unimaginable. Picture a world where a routine doctor's visit includes an AI-powered imaging tool that can detect anomalies invisible to the human eye. These tools, equipped with advanced algorithms, have the extraordinary ability to identify early signs of cancer, providing patients with the opportunity for early intervention. Predictive analytics takes this further by personalizing treatment plans. By analyzing vast datasets from past cases, AI can recommend targeted therapies that enhance outcomes and minimize side effects, tailoring medicine to an individual's genetic profile and lifestyle.

The role of AI in patient monitoring and management extends beyond the doctor's office. Wearable devices, like the young mother's smartwatch, provide real-time health monitoring, offering a wealth of data that informs both patients and healthcare providers. These devices can detect irregularities, prompting timely interventions that prevent minor issues from escalating. For chronic diseases such as diabetes, AI plays a crucial role in management. By analyzing glucose levels, dietary habits, and physical activity, AI systems provide personalized recommendations that help patients maintain control over their conditions, enhancing their quality of life and reducing the risk of complications.

However, the integration of AI in healthcare raises important ethical questions about data use. Patient consent is paramount in the collection and analysis of personal health data. It's essential that patients understand how their data will be used and who will have access to it. Ensuring data privacy and security within electronic health records is also critical. As healthcare systems become more interconnected, protecting sensitive information from breaches becomes a top priority. Transparent algorithms and ethical frameworks must guide the development of AI systems, ensuring they respect patient autonomy and privacy while delivering effective care.

Telemedicine, empowered by AI, is transforming remote healthcare delivery. AI-driven chatbots are often the first point of contact, conducting initial assessments by asking patients about symptoms and medical history. This initial interaction streamlines the process, ensuring that patients receive timely and appropriate care. Virtual health assistants take this further by handling follow-ups and medication reminders, supporting patients in managing their health from the comfort of their homes. These advancements make healthcare more accessible and equitable, particularly for those in remote or underserved areas.

Reflection Exercise: Consider Your Experiences

Reflect on your own experiences with healthcare technology. Have you used any AI-powered tools or devices? How did they impact your healthcare experience? Consider the ethical implications of AI in healthcare—does the use of your data concern you? Write down your thoughts and consider how these technologies might evolve in the future.

AI in healthcare is not just about cutting-edge technology; it's about enhancing patient care and outcomes. By integrating mindfulness principles, we ensure that these advancements serve humanity with empathy and respect. As we continue to explore AI's potential, we must remain vigilant in addressing ethical concerns, ensuring that technology not only advances but also uplifts the human spirit.

Educational Innovations: AI in the Classroom

In classrooms across the world, AI is quietly changing how students learn. Adaptive learning platforms, for instance, tailor educational content to meet each student's unique pace and style. These platforms use complex algorithms to assess how well a student understands a topic and adjust the difficulty of lessons accordingly. Imagine a student struggling with algebra; the AI identifies this challenge and offers additional resources or exercises, ensuring no one is left behind. This personalized approach not only enhances understanding but also boosts confidence, as students engage with material that feels just right for them.

AI doesn't just stop at adapting lessons; it also identifies strengths and areas needing improvement, allowing educators to focus their efforts where they're most needed. This data-driven insight transforms teaching from a one-size-fits-all method to a dynamic, responsive experience.

While AI personalizes learning, it also streamlines administrative tasks, freeing up valuable time for educators. Automated grading systems are a prime example, offering instant feedback on assignments and tests. Teachers no longer have to spend hours marking papers, allowing them to dedicate more energy to developing engaging lesson plans or providing one-on-one support. AI also aids in scheduling and resource allocation, optimizing class timetables and ensuring that educational resources are used efficiently. This efficiency allows schools to focus more on the quality of education and less on logistical headaches, creating a smoother and more effective learning environment for everyone involved.

AI is also a powerful ally in breaking down learning barriers for students with disabilities. Consider speech-to-text applications that assist hearing-impaired students by converting spoken words into text. These tools enable students to follow along in real time, ensuring they don't miss a beat. For ESL learners, AI-driven language translation offers a bridge, making content accessible in the student's native language. This inclusivity fosters a diverse learning environment where every student has the opportunity to succeed, regardless of their language or physical challenges. Such tools exemplify how technology can be harnessed to create a more equitable educational landscape, where diversity is not just acknowledged but celebrated.

Beyond direct interaction with students, AI also supports teachers in their professional development. It identifies areas where educators might benefit from further training, suggesting resources or courses that align with their needs. This targeted approach to professional growth ensures that teachers remain at the forefront of educational innovation, equipped with the skills and knowledge necessary to guide their students effectively. Virtual teaching assistants further support classroom management, handling routine tasks like attendance and basic inquiries. This support allows teachers to focus on creative and impactful teaching strategies, rather than being bogged down by administrative duties.

AI's integration into the classroom is not just about technology for technology's sake. It's about enhancing the educational experience for both students and teachers, creating environments where learning is tailored, efficient, and inclusive. As AI continues to evolve, its potential to transform education grows, promising a future where every student can thrive in a learning environment that truly understands and responds to their needs.

AI and Public Policy: Crafting Mindful Regulations

In the realm of public policy, the integration of AI offers a powerful tool for informed decision-making. By analyzing large datasets, AI can uncover policy insights that were previously hidden within mountains of data. Imagine sifting through years of social and economic data to identify patterns and trends that inform policy decisions—AI makes this possible. Predictive modeling further enhances this capability by allowing policymakers to anticipate social trends and understand potential impacts before they unfold. For instance, AI can model the effects of proposed housing policies on urban development, providing foresight that aids in crafting more effective and equitable regulations. This data-driven approach ensures that policies are not only reactive but proactive, addressing challenges with a precision that manual analysis could never achieve.

Creating robust regulatory frameworks for AI is a critical endeavor that must balance technological innovation with public welfare. International standards for ethical AI use serve as guiding principles, ensuring that AI systems are developed with fairness and accountability in mind. These standards advocate for transparency, requiring that AI algorithms be explainable and decisions traceable. National AI strategies often build on these international guidelines, tailoring them to reflect local needs and values. Implementing these strategies involves crafting laws and regulations that protect citizens while fostering innovation. Policymakers face the challenge of setting boundaries that prevent misuse without stifling AI's potential to drive progress.

AI also plays a pivotal role in enhancing public engagement and transparency within policy discussions. Tools for public sentiment analysis allow policymakers to gauge public opinion on various issues quickly and efficiently. By analyzing social media trends and public forums, AI can identify prevalent concerns and areas where policy interventions are needed. This real-time feedback loop empowers governments to respond to public needs more dynamically. Virtual town halls, facilitated by AI, bring an innovative dimension to public engagement. These platforms enable real-time interaction between citizens and policymakers, breaking down barriers to participation and fostering a more inclusive democratic process. The immediacy and accessibility of virtual town halls ensure that diverse voices are heard and considered in policy formulation.

Despite these advancements, integrating AI into policy frameworks presents notable challenges. One of the primary obstacles is balancing innovation with regulation. While AI offers immense potential, unregulated use can lead to unintended consequences, such as bias or privacy violations. Policymakers must tread carefully, crafting regulations that promote ethical AI use without hindering technological advancement. Addressing digital divides in policy access is another significant challenge. Not all communities have equal access to the digital tools necessary for participating in AI-driven policy processes. Ensuring that rural or underserved populations are not left behind requires deliberate strategies, such as investing in digital infrastructure and literacy programs that bridge these gaps.

In this complex landscape, crafting mindful regulations for AI demands a nuanced approach that considers ethical, social, and technological dimensions. By leveraging AI's capabilities in data analysis and public engagement, policymakers can craft regulations that not only govern AI use but also harness its potential to enhance public welfare. This approach ensures that as AI continues to evolve, its integration into public policy remains aligned with the principles of justice and equity, fostering a future where technology serves all members of society.

Ethical AI in Finance and Business

In the fast-paced world of finance, AI has introduced transformative changes, particularly in risk management and fraud detection. Imagine a system capable of monitoring countless transactions in real-time, flagging suspicious activity faster than any human analyst could. AI's ability to process vast amounts of data instantly allows financial institutions to detect fraudulent activities before they escalate into major issues. By analyzing transaction patterns and identifying anomalies, AI systems can prevent fraud, helping to protect both institutions and consumers.

AI is also proving invaluable in credit scoring and risk assessment. Traditional credit assessments often rely on static data, such as past credit history. In contrast, AI can incorporate dynamic, real-time information, providing a more nuanced view of a borrower's reliability. This advancement not only reduces default rates but also expands access to credit for individuals who may have been overlooked by traditional models.

Another area where AI is making a significant impact is the personalization of financial services. Robo-advisors are leading the way by offering investment advice tailored to individual risk profiles and financial goals. These AI-driven advisors analyze market trends, personal data, and investment patterns to provide recommendations that are both personalized and timely. This approach also extends to loan offers and terms, with AI systems assessing a borrower's unique circumstances to propose loans that align with their needs and financial capabilities. The result is twofold: consumers receive services better suited to their situations, while financial institutions build stronger customer relationships, leading to higher satisfaction and loyalty.

AI's influence also extends to operational efficiency and cost reduction in business operations. By automating routine tasks, AI reduces overhead costs and allows human workers to focus on more complex, value-added activities. In the supply chain, for example, AI algorithms optimize inventory levels, predict demand fluctuations, and streamline logistics. This optimization cuts costs while enhancing business agility and responsiveness, enabling companies to quickly adapt to market changes. The result is a more efficient operation that delivers products and services faster, meeting consumer demands with precision and reliability.

However, the integration of AI in finance and business must be approached with careful consideration of ethical implications, particularly regarding consumer trust and transparency. Transparent AI algorithms are essential for ensuring fairness and accountability in financial decisions. Consumers need to understand how AI systems make decisions that impact their finances, whether it's approving a loan or providing investment advice. This transparency fosters trust, reassuring consumers that AI-driven financial services are designed with their best interests in mind.

Ensuring fairness in automated financial decisions is also crucial. AI systems must be regularly audited and updated to prevent bias, ensuring that all consumers are treated equitably and that decisions do not disproportionately affect specific groups.

As AI technology continues to evolve, its role in finance and business will undoubtedly expand. The challenge and opportunity lies in leveraging AI's capabilities to enhance financial security, personalize services, optimize operations, and maintain consumer trust, all while adhering to ethical standards. Striking the right balance between innovation and ethics will define the future of AI in finance, creating a system that not only serves but also empowers individuals and businesses alike.

AI's Impact on Environmental Sustainability

AI's potential to revolutionize environmental sustainability is both vast and promising. In agriculture, AI applications are making significant strides in resource management. Consider water usage, a critical issue in farming that directly impacts both crop yield and environmental conservation. AI systems equipped with sensors and predictive algorithms optimize irrigation practices by analyzing soil moisture, weather forecasts, and crop needs. This technology ensures that water is used efficiently, reducing waste and preserving this precious resource. Farmers can now make informed decisions about when and how much to water their crops, leading to healthier yields and more sustainable agricultural practices.

Fishing, another vital industry, benefits from AI's predictive modeling capabilities. Sustainable fishing practices are essential to maintaining marine biodiversity and ensuring long-term viability. AI systems analyze data from satellite imagery and marine sensors to predict fish movements and population dynamics. By understanding these patterns, fisheries can avoid overfishing, protect endangered species, and optimize their harvests. This balance supports both the fishing industry and the health of marine ecosystems, demonstrating AI's crucial role in fostering sustainable resource management.

Climate change mitigation is another area where AI's impact is profound. Accurate climate predictions are vital for developing effective strategies to combat climate change. AI models analyze vast datasets, including historical weather patterns and current environmental conditions, to predict climate trends and extreme weather events. These insights enable governments and organizations to prepare for and respond to natural disasters, minimizing their impact on communities.

Additionally, AI-driven energy consumption optimization in buildings is transforming urban landscapes. By analyzing data from smart meters and IoT devices, AI systems adjust heating, cooling, and lighting in real-time, reducing energy waste and carbon footprints. This intelligent management of energy resources is essential in the global effort to reduce greenhouse gas emissions and combat climate change.

When it comes to waste reduction and recycling, AI offers innovative solutions that enhance efficiency and effectiveness. In sorting facilities, AI-powered robots use machine learning algorithms and computer vision to identify and separate different types of materials. This precise sorting reduces contamination and improves recycling rates, ensuring that more materials are reused rather than sent to landfills. Predictive analytics further aid in waste management by forecasting waste generation patterns. By understanding these patterns, municipalities can optimize waste collection schedules and allocate resources more effectively, reducing costs and improving service quality.

Biodiversity and conservation efforts also benefit significantly from AI technologies. Tracking and monitoring wildlife populations are critical for understanding species' health and behavior, especially those at risk of extinction. AI systems analyze data from camera traps, drones, and satellites to monitor animal movements and habitat use.

This information helps conservationists and researchers develop strategies to protect endangered species and preserve natural habitats.

Remote sensing technologies, powered by AI, provide real-time data on habitat changes, such as deforestation or urban expansion. These insights are crucial for implementing conservation measures that protect biodiversity and maintain ecological balance.

In this exploration of AI's role in environmental sustainability, it becomes clear that technology can be a powerful ally in our efforts to preserve the planet. By optimizing resource management, mitigating climate change, reducing waste, and supporting conservation, AI offers solutions that align with our responsibility to protect and sustain the environment for future generations. As we continue to integrate AI into these efforts, we must remain mindful of ethical considerations, ensuring that these technologies serve as tools for positive change. With AI's support, we can strive toward a more sustainable and equitable world, where the environment and technology coexist in harmony.

CHAPTER 5
Developing Mindful AI Systems

"Mindfulness asks us to be aware of our biases, and AI development should follow the same path—ensuring that its algorithms are unbiased and open to growth."

Mindfulness encourages us to be aware of our biases, and AI development should follow a similar path—ensuring that its algorithms remain unbiased and adaptable to growth.

Imagine standing in a lively city park, surrounded by the hum of conversations and laughter. Nearby, an interactive art installation catches your eye. It's an AI system that responds to the emotions of those around it, adjusting its colors and sounds based on the collective mood. This captivating piece is not just a technological marvel; it's a reflection of intentional, thoughtful AI development. It embodies a conscious effort to create technology that connects with human emotions and enhances shared experiences. This scenario highlights a crucial element of AI development: the importance of setting clear, purposeful goals rooted in mindful principles.

Clear objectives are the foundation of any successful AI project. It's about defining your goals with precision and intention. These objectives should align with your organization's core values, ensuring that the technology you create enhances your broader mission and vision. Engaging stakeholders in the goal-setting process is essential. Their diverse perspectives can uncover potential challenges and opportunities, offering a well-rounded view that guides the project's direction. By integrating stakeholder input, you create a sense of shared ownership, fostering collaboration and innovation. This approach ensures that the project stays aligned with organizational values while meeting the needs of those it aims to serve.

Looking toward the future of AI involves establishing a long-term vision that considers its societal impact. Anticipating technological shifts helps you foresee how AI will evolve and integrate into everyday life. This foresight allows you to strike a balance between innovation and ethical considerations, ensuring that AI systems make a positive contribution to society. By taking a broader perspective, you can design AI that is not only advanced but also socially responsible. This long-term vision helps you navigate the complexities of AI development, making decisions that prioritize both progress and ethical integrity. It encourages you to think beyond immediate outcomes, considering how today's innovations will shape tomorrow's world.

Consider the case of AI initiatives in sustainable development, where intentional goal-setting has led to significant societal benefits. Projects that integrate AI into environmental conservation have successfully balanced technological innovation with ecological preservation. By setting clear objectives that prioritize sustainability, these initiatives have developed AI systems to monitor and protect natural resources. Similarly, educational AI tools, designed with a long-term vision of enhancing learning outcomes, have transformed classrooms. By aligning goals with educational values, these tools provide personalized learning experiences catering to diverse student needs. These examples demonstrate the transformative potential of intentional goal-setting in AI development, offering insights to guide your own projects.

Reflection Exercise: Setting Your AI Goals

Take a moment to reflect on an AI project you're currently working on or planning. Write down the core objectives and consider how they align with your organizational values. Are these goals diverse enough to include stakeholder perspectives? Think about the long-term vision for this project. How will it impact society, and what ethical implications might arise? Use this reflection to clarify your intentions and guide the development process.

As you explore these concepts, remember that setting intentional goals is not just a strategic exercise but a fundamental aspect of developing AI that respects and enhances human values. By prioritizing clear objectives, long-term vision, and iterative assessment, you can create AI systems that are both innovative and mindful, serving as partners in our collective journey toward a better future.

Integrating Compassionate Algorithms

Picture the bustling environment of a modern-day call center, where AI-powered customer service bots are at work. These bots aren't just automated responders; they're designed with empathy, capable of understanding and responding to human emotions. By incorporating human-centered design principles, these algorithms prioritize empathy and user welfare. The process begins with empathy mapping in algorithm development, where developers imagine the customer's perspective, considering their needs, emotions, and potential frustrations. This approach transforms a simple transactional interaction into a compassionate exchange, enhancing the overall user experience.

The techniques to integrate compassion into AI systems are both innovative and practical. Sentiment analysis is a powerful tool that allows AI to gauge user emotions through language cues, tone, and context. By analyzing text or voice inputs, AI can detect whether a user is frustrated, confused, or satisfied. This emotional intelligence enables the AI to tailor its responses accordingly, offering reassurance, clarity, or appreciation as needed. Adaptive learning algorithms also play a crucial role in responding to user needs. These algorithms learn from each interaction, refining their responses over time to better meet user expectations. This adaptability ensures that AI systems remain relevant and responsive, continuously improving the user experience.

The impact of compassionate algorithms on user experience is profound. Personalized interactions create a sense of connection, making users feel understood and valued. When AI systems respond with empathy, they reduce user frustration, turning potential challenges into opportunities for positive engagement. For instance, if a customer struggles with a product issue, a compassionate AI bot can not only provide a solution but also acknowledge the customer's frustration empathetically. This approach builds trust and loyalty, encouraging users to engage with the technology confidently and willingly.

Real-world applications of compassionate algorithms demonstrate their potential to enhance various sectors. In mental health support, AI systems equipped with emotional recognition capabilities provide invaluable assistance. These systems analyze vocal patterns and language to assess a user's emotional state, offering support and tailored resources.

Such applications are particularly beneficial for individuals hesitant to seek help in traditional settings, providing a safe and accessible avenue for mental health care. In customer service, AI bots with emotional recognition capabilities transform interactions by recognizing and responding to customer emotions in real time. This ability to empathize allows companies to address concerns more effectively, enhancing customer satisfaction and retention.

Compassionate algorithms are revolutionizing how we interact with technology, creating systems that meet functional needs while resonating on a human level. As we continue to develop and refine these technologies, the focus remains on enhancing user experience through empathy and understanding. By embedding compassion into the core of AI systems, we create technology that truly serves humanity, fostering connections that transcend the digital divide.

Designing for Mindful User Experiences

Envision interacting with an AI as intuitive as talking to an old friend. This captures the essence of user-centric design in AI development. It begins with creating interfaces that are both functional and intuitive, allowing users to navigate them effortlessly. Intuitive interfaces combine aesthetics with practicality, guiding users smoothly without unnecessary complexity. Picture a smartphone app that anticipates your needs, offering clear options without overwhelming choices. Achieving this requires a deep understanding of the user journey, anticipating needs, and addressing potential frustrations.

Accessibility is a fundamental aspect of mindful design. AI systems must be inclusive, accommodating a wide range of users with diverse needs and abilities. This means interfaces should be easy to use and adaptable for individuals with disabilities. Features such as voice recognition, adjustable text sizes, and alternative input methods help make technology accessible to everyone. Designing for accessibility empowers users, breaking down barriers and promoting equality. It's not just a technical requirement—it's a commitment to diversity and inclusion.

Mindful interaction models enhance user experiences by fostering meaningful, engaging connections. Interactive storytelling, for instance, makes users a part of the narrative, allowing them to influence outcomes. Visualize an educational app teaching history through storytelling, where students explore different eras and make decisions that shape the storyline. This approach makes learning more memorable and impactful. Feedback mechanisms also play a key role by encouraging reflection, prompting users to consider their actions within the AI environment.

User testing and feedback are essential in refining AI experiences. Iterative design involves continuous testing and tweaking based on user input to ensure the final product meets expectations. Workshops and focus groups reveal how AI systems perform in real-world scenarios. These sessions provide a platform for users to voice opinions and suggest improvements, fostering a collaborative process. By involving users, developers create systems that resonate with their audience, building trust and connection.

Gamified AI educational tools blend learning and play, creating engaging, interactive experiences. They use game mechanics to motivate students, making education enjoyable and effective. Similarly, AI-driven wellness apps promote mindfulness by encouraging users to reflect on their mental and physical well-being. These apps offer personalized insights, helping users adopt healthier habits. Mindful design enhances engagement, creating experiences that are both meaningful and transformative.

Designing mindful user experiences goes beyond aesthetics and functionality. It's about connecting with users on a human level, understanding their needs, and enriching their lives. User-centric design, accessibility, and mindful interactions transform AI systems from tools into partners, supporting well-being and fostering positive change. Thoughtful design ensures AI becomes a catalyst for human-centered innovation, bridging the gap between technology and meaningful connection.

Strategies for Continuous Ethical Evaluation

In a vibrant tech hub where AI evolves rapidly, ensuring ethical integrity is not a one-time task but an ongoing commitment. Ethical evaluation frameworks provide structure, allowing for regular assessments of AI's societal impacts. Audits and compliance checks serve as the backbone, systematically reviewing processes to ensure alignment with ethical standards. These assessments critically examine how AI aligns with values and expectations, going beyond checklists to evaluate broader implications.

Diverse stakeholders play a crucial role in enriching ethical evaluations by offering varied perspectives and insights. Community consultations provide inclusive viewpoints, reflecting the needs of those directly affected. Cross-disciplinary ethical review boards, consisting of technologists, ethicists, psychologists, and policymakers, foster a comprehensive approach. These boards consider the ethical, technical, and social dimensions, ensuring AI systems align with societal norms.

Feedback and adaptation are vital in maintaining ethical integrity. This involves gathering insights, implementing changes, and monitoring systems for compliance. Corrective measures might include retraining algorithms or refining datasets to address concerns. Continuous monitoring ensures adaptability to evolving ethical landscapes and societal expectations. This process keeps AI systems responsive and relevant in a world where norms shift alongside technological advancements.

Leading organizations showcase best practices. Dedicated ethics teams work alongside developers to integrate ethics at every stage. Regular reviews ensure AI is both innovative and aligned with human values. Government initiatives also play a role, setting standards through regulations that promote transparency, accountability, and fairness. These efforts highlight the importance of embedding ethics into the core of AI development.

Developing ethically sound AI is an ongoing process. By establishing robust frameworks, engaging stakeholders, and remaining open to feedback, organizations ensure AI contributes positively to society. This approach fosters trust, accountability, and progress, demonstrating that technology and ethics can coexist harmoniously.

Building Adaptive AI with Human Values

Incorporating human values into AI is like weaving empathy into technology. Value-sensitive design integrates ethics at every stage of development, ensuring systems align with moral and cultural norms. Collaborating with ethicists and social scientists enriches this process, offering insights into human behavior and societal dynamics. These perspectives guide developers in creating systems that enhance, rather than disrupt, lives.

Adaptive learning systems showcase AI's ability to evolve. These systems learn from user interactions, refining responses and functionalities through feedback. Self-learning algorithms enable real-time adaptability, ensuring relevance in a changing world. Adaptive systems can respond to cultural shifts, addressing diverse user needs and fostering inclusivity. This adaptability bridges cultural gaps, creating universally resonant experiences.

Challenges exist in creating adaptive AI. Balancing adaptability with predictability is complex; systems must respond to new contexts without becoming uncontrollable. Ethical alignment in evolving systems is critical, requiring continuous oversight to prevent harm or bias. Developers must ensure flexibility while upholding ethical standards, navigating these challenges to create responsible systems.

Successful implementations highlight adaptive AI's potential. In education, systems tailor lessons to individual needs, optimizing learning outcomes. In healthcare, adaptive AI refines treatment plans using real-time patient data, enhancing care. These systems demonstrate how adaptability can transform industries, fostering innovation while prioritizing human values.

As we delve deeper into integrating human values and adaptability in AI, it becomes evident that these systems can revolutionize our relationship with technology. By prioritizing ethics and embracing adaptability, we can develop AI that is not only innovative but also attuned to the values and needs of the societies it serves. Such systems have the power to enrich our lives, fostering connections that transcend technological boundaries and resonate with our shared humanity.

CHAPTER 6

The Future of AI and Mindfulness

"The intersection of mindfulness and AI reminds us that technology is not separate from us. It is a reflection of our collective consciousness and actions."

Picture a bustling city street where autonomous vehicles glide seamlessly alongside pedestrians, each car navigating with precision and safety. This isn't a far-off dream; it's a glimpse into a future shaped by the rapid evolution of artificial intelligence. As we stand on the brink of this transformative era, understanding the trends and innovations that will define AI's future becomes not just fascinating but essential.

Autonomous systems are steadily becoming a staple of modern life. From self-driving cars to drones delivering packages, these technologies promise to revolutionize transportation and logistics, offering efficiency and safety. The growth of AI in autonomous systems reflects a broader trend in which machines increasingly perform tasks traditionally carried out by humans, creating new opportunities and challenges.

In the realm of healthcare, the expansion of AI into personalized medicine is particularly exciting. Imagine doctors using AI to analyze genetic data, tailoring treatments with unprecedented precision. AI-driven tools can predict how patients will respond to different medications, minimizing adverse effects and maximizing efficacy. This personalized approach is transforming healthcare, offering the potential to drastically improve outcomes and reduce costs.

As AI continues to evolve, its role in creative industries is also expanding. AI-driven creative processes are enabling artists and designers to push boundaries, generating novel works of art, music, and literature. These tools offer inspiration and collaboration, challenging traditional notions of creativity and authorship.

Looking ahead, several technological innovations are poised to reshape AI capabilities even further. Quantum computing, for instance, holds the promise of exponentially increasing AI's computational power. By leveraging the principles of quantum mechanics, these computers can solve complex problems that are currently beyond reach. This breakthrough is expected to accelerate AI development, opening new frontiers in fields like cryptography and drug discovery.

Meanwhile, the rise of edge AI is transforming how data is processed. Unlike traditional AI, which relies on centralized data centers, edge AI processes data locally on devices. This shift reduces latency, enhances privacy, and enables real-time decision-making, making it ideal for applications like smart cities and the Internet of Things.

AI's influence is extending into emerging fields, bringing with it the potential for groundbreaking discoveries. In space exploration, AI is being used to analyze vast amounts of data from telescopes and satellites, helping scientists understand our universe better. AI algorithms can identify patterns in cosmic data, revealing insights that may have otherwise gone unnoticed.

Similarly, in bioinformatics and genetic research, AI is revolutionizing how we study biological systems. By analyzing genetic sequences and biological data, AI can identify potential targets for new drugs and therapies, accelerating the pace of biomedical innovation. These applications highlight AI's potential to drive scientific advancements and improve human life on a global scale.

Yet, with these advancements come challenges that demand careful consideration. The ethical implications of AI in surveillance technologies, for example, raise concerns about privacy and civil liberties. As AI becomes more capable of monitoring and analyzing human behavior, ensuring that these technologies are used responsibly is paramount. Policymakers and technologists must collaborate to establish frameworks that protect individual rights while leveraging AI's benefits.

On the other hand, AI presents opportunities to enhance global connectivity, bridging gaps between communities and fostering collaboration across borders. By facilitating communication and data sharing, AI can help address global challenges like climate change and infectious diseases, promoting a more interconnected and resilient world.

Reflection Section: Embracing AI's Future

Think about how AI's evolution might impact your field. Consider the trends highlighted in this chapter and reflect on how they could reshape your work, community, or industry. Are there innovations you're particularly excited about? Are there challenges you foresee? Write down your thoughts and explore how you might prepare for and contribute to this evolving landscape.

6.2 The Role of Mindfulness in AI's Future

Imagine a world where AI systems don't just function mechanically but operate with a sense of intentionality, akin to a thoughtful human collaborator. Mindfulness principles can guide the development of such AI systems, ensuring that they act with purpose and consideration. By emphasizing intentionality in AI design, developers can create algorithms that not only perform tasks efficiently but also align with ethical standards and human values.

This involves embedding compassion into AI algorithms, allowing machines to understand and respond to human emotions in a way that feels empathetic and supportive. For instance, consider an AI in healthcare that not only diagnoses but also delivers bad news with sensitivity, offering supportive resources and follow-ups. Such AI systems can transform user experiences, making interactions with technology feel more human and less transactional.

Mindfulness isn't just a tool for development; it can also serve as a framework for regulating AI. By informing ethical standards with mindfulness principles, we can establish guidelines that prioritize human well-being and ethical integrity. This approach is not purely theoretical. Mindfulness-based policy development has shown promise in various sectors, offering a model for crafting regulations that balance technological advancement with societal good.

Policymakers can draw on these examples to ensure AI systems operate transparently, accountably, and fairly, mitigating risks associated with bias and misuse. The application of mindfulness as a regulatory framework ensures that AI not only complies with legal requirements but also contributes positively to society.

Cultural integration of mindfulness into AI development and deployment offers another layer of depth. Different cultures interpret and practice mindfulness in unique ways, providing a rich tapestry of traditions that can inform AI design. By adapting mindfulness principles to local contexts, developers can create AI systems that resonate with diverse user groups, enhancing their relevance and acceptance.

Global mindfulness initiatives in AI promote cross-cultural understanding and cooperation. These initiatives encourage the sharing of best practices and insights, fostering a global community committed to ethical and mindful AI development. This cultural integration enriches AI systems, making them more adaptable and effective across various societal contexts.

The long-term impacts of a mindful approach to AI are profound, offering potential benefits that extend beyond immediate technological gains. By reducing societal stress associated with AI, such as privacy concerns and job displacement, mindfulness can cultivate a more harmonious relationship between humans and machines.

This approach emphasizes the importance of designing AI systems that support mental health and well-being, reducing anxiety and enhancing daily life. Moreover, mindful AI practices can promote global cooperation. By encouraging collaboration and dialogue, these practices can help bridge divides and foster a shared vision for the future of technology.

As we integrate mindfulness into AI, we create opportunities for collective growth and understanding, paving the way for a future where technology enhances, rather than detracts from, our humanity.

6.3 Preparing for AI-Driven Job Market Changes

Imagine a bustling office, once filled with the hum of human activity, now transformed by AI automation. Routine tasks, from data entry to scheduling, are seamlessly managed by intelligent systems. This shift is not just about efficiency; it represents a fundamental change in the job market landscape. As AI takes on repetitive tasks, industries are witnessing a transformation where new roles emerge, demanding skills beyond automation's reach. You might find yourself navigating this evolving terrain, where adaptability becomes your greatest asset. The rise of new AI-related job roles, such as AI ethicists, data analysts, and machine learning specialists, highlights the need for a workforce keen on innovation and ethical considerations.

In this AI-driven market, creativity and critical thinking have never been more crucial. As machines handle routine processes, your ability to think outside the box and solve complex problems becomes invaluable. Organizations will increasingly seek individuals who can bring fresh ideas and navigate the ethical complexities of AI implementation. Alongside these skills, emotional intelligence and interpersonal abilities gain prominence. While AI excels in data processing, it lacks the nuanced understanding of human emotions and relationships. Your capability to empathize, communicate, and collaborate will set you apart, fostering a workplace environment where human strengths complement AI's capabilities.

Navigating career transitions in this dynamic landscape requires a mindful approach. Embrace lifelong learning as a constant companion, allowing you to adapt and thrive amid change. Continuously updating your skills ensures you remain relevant, whether through formal education or self-directed learning. Consider career planning through a mindful lens, where resilience and adaptability guide your decisions. Stay informed about industry trends, explore new opportunities, and embrace change with an open mind. This proactive approach not only prepares you for shifts in the job market but also empowers you to shape your career path with intention and purpose.

Policy and support systems play a pivotal role in facilitating these transitions. Government initiatives focused on retraining and upskilling provide valuable resources as you navigate new career landscapes. These programs, designed to equip you with in-demand skills, are crucial in bridging the gap between traditional roles and emerging opportunities. Industry partnerships further enhance workforce adaptation, as companies collaborate to create training programs aligned with market needs. By participating in these initiatives, you gain access to networks and knowledge that support your growth and adaptation. As you embrace this AI-driven future, remember that you are not alone; a supportive ecosystem surrounds you, ready to guide and uplift your journey.

In this evolving landscape, the convergence of AI and human potential offers a world of possibilities. While AI automates tasks and creates efficiencies, it also opens doors to roles that demand creativity, empathy, and innovation. By cultivating these skills and embracing change, you position yourself to thrive in the job market of tomorrow. As you navigate this path, draw on your strengths, seek out resources, and engage with communities that share your vision for a future where technology enhances human potential.

6.4 Balancing Technological Advancement with Human Well-Being

In the bustling world of AI, the focus often gravitates toward innovation and efficiency. Yet, the true measure of success lies in how these advancements enhance human well-being. Human-centric AI design places individuals at the heart of technological development. This approach emphasizes intuitive interfaces that empower users, ensuring that interactions with AI are seamless and enriching. Consider a digital assistant that learns your preferences over time, offering tailored suggestions that improve daily life. Whether it's reminding you to take a break or suggesting a new hobby, such intuitive design elevates user experience, making technology a supportive partner rather than just a tool. Moreover, assistive technologies harness AI's potential to enhance the quality of life for those with disabilities, offering new ways to navigate and interact with the world around them.

Ethical considerations in AI development are paramount, especially as we explore new frontiers. Technology addiction and over-reliance represent significant pitfalls. In an age where devices constantly vie for our attention, it's easy to become too dependent on technology. AI systems must be designed to promote healthy usage patterns, encouraging breaks and fostering offline interaction. Equitable access to AI benefits is another critical ethical issue. As AI becomes more integrated into society, ensuring that all individuals, regardless of socioeconomic status, can access and benefit from these technologies is crucial. This requires a conscious effort to address digital divides and create inclusive systems that serve diverse populations.

AI's role in supporting mental health and well-being is becoming increasingly significant. Innovative AI tools offer stress management solutions, providing users with personalized relaxation techniques and mindfulness exercises. These applications can track stress levels and suggest interventions, helping users maintain emotional balance. AI also promotes social well-being by connecting people who might otherwise feel isolated. Virtual communities and social platforms powered by AI enable individuals to find support and build meaningful relationships. These tools facilitate connection and communication, enhancing social networks and fostering a sense of belonging.

A closer look at case studies reveals initiatives that successfully balance technology with well-being. In the workplace, AI-driven wellness programs offer insights into employee health, suggesting personalized interventions to boost productivity and morale. These programs might recommend ergonomic adjustments or encourage regular breaks, helping employees maintain physical and mental health. Meanwhile, smart city projects leverage AI to create urban environments that enhance quality of life. By optimizing traffic flow, reducing pollution, and improving public safety, these projects demonstrate AI's potential to transform cities into livable, sustainable spaces. These examples illustrate how the thoughtful integration of AI can lead to environments that prioritize human well-being.

By focusing on human-centric design and ethical innovation, AI can truly enhance our lives. The key lies in crafting technologies that respect and support our needs, ensuring that AI advancements contribute positively to society.

6.5 Envisioning a Mindful Technological Ecosystem

Picture a room filled with diverse voices, each contributing unique perspectives on the future of technology. This is the essence of collaborative visioning. By engaging stakeholders across various fields, we can collectively shape a technological ecosystem that prioritizes both innovation and inclusivity. Workshops designed for collective future planning serve as fertile ground for ideas to flourish. Here, technologists, ethicists, psychologists, educators, and policymakers gather to brainstorm and co-create solutions that are not only innovative but also holistic. These cross-disciplinary collaborations ensure that the resulting technologies address complex societal needs comprehensively, reflecting the wisdom of multiple disciplines working in harmony.

Building inclusive ecosystems is not merely a goal; it is a necessity for the future of technology. As we design systems that cater to diverse user needs and experiences, we create a space where technology serves everyone, regardless of their background or abilities. This involves ensuring representation within AI development teams, bringing together individuals from various demographics and areas of expertise. Such diversity enriches the development process, fostering creativity and empathy in design. It also helps prevent biases, ensuring that the technologies we create are fair and beneficial for all. Inclusivity in technology is about recognizing and valuing every voice, making sure that no one is left behind as we advance.

Mindfulness and sustainability go hand in hand, offering a pathway to reduce the environmental impact of technology. By promoting mindful AI use, we can develop systems that are efficient and environmentally friendly. This involves designing AI that optimizes resource usage, minimizing waste and energy consumption. Encouraging the responsible consumption of technology is equally important. Just as mindfulness teaches us to be present and intentional in our actions, we can apply these principles to how we engage with technology. By being conscious of our tech usage, we can reduce unnecessary consumption, leading to a more sustainable relationship with the tools we rely on daily.

Practical pathways to achieve a mindful tech ecosystem are within reach. Policy frameworks play a crucial role in supporting sustainable tech development, providing guidelines and incentives for organizations to adopt mindful practices. These frameworks can encourage the development of technologies that prioritize sustainability and ethical considerations. Community-driven initiatives further enrich this landscape, as grassroots movements promote mindful tech adoption and use. By engaging local communities in the conversation, we foster a sense of ownership and responsibility, empowering individuals to make informed choices about their technological interactions. These initiatives demonstrate that change is possible at both the individual and collective levels.

As we envision a mindful technological ecosystem, we lay the groundwork for a future where technology and humanity coexist in harmony. This chapter highlights the importance of collaboration, inclusivity, and sustainability, offering a roadmap to a future where technology enhances our lives without compromising our values. In the next chapter, we will explore how these principles can be applied to real-world scenarios, illustrating the transformative potential of a mindful approach to technology.

CHAPTER 7
Interdisciplinary Perspectives on AI

"As we teach AI to learn, we should also teach it to reflect, observe, and be conscious of its surroundings—just as mindfulness teaches humans to be present and aware."

Picture a bustling university campus, where students interact with intelligent kiosks that guide them through the day. These kiosks don't just dispense information; they engage, understand, and adapt based on each student's needs and moods. This scenario underscores the potential of AI when psychology and technology come together. The intersection of these fields unlocks new dimensions of user experience, offering systems that are not only functional but also empathetic and responsive.

Bridging Technology and Psychology in AI Design

Understanding human-centric AI design begins with recognizing the role of psychological principles in crafting user experiences. Human-centered AI (HCAI) is a framework that prioritizes human needs, values, and capabilities, aiming to augment rather than replace human roles (Source 1). By integrating psychology into AI design, we can address cognitive load—the mental effort required to use a system. User interfaces become more intuitive when they consider how users process information, reducing unnecessary complexity and enhancing interaction ease. For example, an AI-driven scheduling app that anticipates your needs before you realize them can streamline your day, freeing up mental resources for more creative tasks.

Behavioral insights play a crucial role in AI engagement strategies. These insights help AI systems understand user motivations and preferences, leading to more personalized and satisfying interactions. Consider an AI-powered learning platform that adapts content delivery based on how students engage with materials, fostering a more effective and enjoyable learning experience. By understanding user behavior, AI can tailor interactions, making them more meaningful and less intrusive.

Emotional AI takes this integration further by embedding emotional intelligence into systems. Emotion recognition algorithms allow AI to detect and interpret human emotions, providing responses that are empathetic and appropriate. Imagine a virtual customer service agent that can sense frustration and adjust its tone and approach accordingly, turning a potentially negative interaction into a positive experience. These systems can respond to emotional states in real-time, enhancing user satisfaction and loyalty.

Building trust in AI technologies is paramount, and psychological strategies offer valuable tools for fostering this trust. Transparency in AI processes and decision-making is crucial. When users understand how an AI system works and makes decisions, they are more likely to trust its outputs. Additionally, consistent and reliable AI interactions reinforce user confidence. If an AI assistant reliably manages your calendar without errors, you're more likely to rely on it for increasingly complex tasks.

Successful case studies illustrate the power of integrating psychology into AI. AI-driven mental wellness applications provide support and therapy, offering users a non-judgmental space to explore emotions and build resilience. These applications leverage psychological principles to guide users through structured exercises, promoting mental health and well-being. In robotics, social robots designed with psychological insights engage users in meaningful interactions. These robots can serve as companions for the elderly, reducing loneliness by providing a sense of presence and understanding.

Reflection Exercise: Evaluating Emotional AI

Reflect on a recent interaction with an AI system. Consider how the system addressed your cognitive load and emotional needs. Did it respond appropriately to your mood or preferences? How did this affect your trust in the technology? Jot down your observations and think about how these insights could inform future AI designs.

As you explore these interdisciplinary perspectives, consider how the fusion of technology and psychology can redefine AI's role in our lives. This synergy has the potential to create systems that not only meet functional needs but also enrich human experiences, fostering deeper connections and understanding.

Ethical Implications from a Philosophical Standpoint

When we think about the philosophical foundations of AI ethics, we encounter a rich tapestry of theories that guide the creation and deployment of artificial intelligence. Utilitarianism, for instance, is a principle that suggests the best action is the one that maximizes overall happiness. In AI, this translates to decision-making processes that aim to produce the greatest good for the greatest number. Imagine an AI system in a healthcare setting that prioritizes treatments based on potential outcomes, maximizing health benefits across the patient population. Utilitarianism in AI pushes us to consider the broader impact of technological decisions, ensuring they align with collective well-being.

Deontological ethics offers another lens, focusing on adhering to moral rules or duties regardless of the outcome. This approach is integral when setting rules for AI behavior, particularly in scenarios where the consequences of actions are uncertain. An autonomous vehicle, for example, might be programmed with strict adherence to traffic laws, even when breaking them could potentially avoid an accident. By emphasizing rules and duties, deontological ethics provides a framework for AI that values consistency and moral integrity, even when outcomes aren't ideal.

Virtue ethics shifts the focus from rules and outcomes to the moral character of the decision-maker—in this case, the AI system. Here, the question isn't just about what action to take, but what kind of AI we want to create. This approach encourages developers to imbue AI with virtues like honesty, compassion, and fairness, creating systems that reflect the best of human character. In practice, this could mean designing AI decision-support systems in healthcare that prioritize empathetic patient interactions alongside clinical efficiency, embodying a balance of technical proficiency and moral sensitivity.

The concept of moral agency becomes relevant as we consider AI systems that operate with increasing autonomy. Moral agency refers to the capacity to make ethical decisions and be held accountable for them. In autonomous systems, defining moral agency is complex. Are these systems acting as independent agents or merely tools executing pre-programmed commands? This distinction is crucial in determining responsibility and accountability. The debate over AI as moral agents challenges us to rethink accountability frameworks, ensuring that both developers and AI systems share responsibility for ethical outcomes.

Ethical dilemmas in AI often mirror classic philosophical paradoxes. The trolley problem, a thought experiment where a person must decide whether to divert a train to save lives at the cost of another, finds new relevance in autonomous vehicles. These vehicles might face decisions about who to prioritize in unavoidable accidents, prompting discussions about programming ethics and responsibility. Similarly, the balance between privacy and utility in data-driven AI poses significant ethical questions. Collecting data enhances AI's utility but risks infringing on individual privacy. Finding this balance is a philosophical challenge that requires careful consideration of ethical priorities.

Real-world applications demonstrate how philosophical ethics inform AI practices. In military contexts, AI must navigate ethical considerations around autonomous weaponry, balancing national security with humanitarian concerns. These applications demand rigorous ethical scrutiny to ensure compliance with international laws and moral standards. In healthcare, AI decision-support systems must balance data-driven recommendations with patient autonomy and consent. These systems exemplify the practical integration of philosophical ethics, guiding technology toward outcomes that respect human dignity and ethical principles.

AI, Education, and Social Impact

Imagine walking into a classroom where each student is greeted by a personalized AI tutor that knows exactly how to help them succeed. This is the transformative potential of AI in education. Personalized learning pathways powered by AI allow students to progress at their own pace, focusing on their unique strengths and addressing their challenges. No longer bound by the one-size-fits-all approach, education becomes a tailored journey. AI tools facilitate differentiated instruction, adapting content to meet diverse learning styles and needs. This flexibility not only enhances understanding but also empowers students to take ownership of their learning, fostering deeper engagement with the material. Teachers also benefit as AI alleviates administrative burdens, allowing them to focus more on direct student interaction and creative lesson planning.

However, the promise of AI in education extends beyond personalized learning. It plays a crucial role in promoting social equity and access. In regions where educational resources are scarce, AI can bridge gaps by providing access to quality education. Online platforms and AI-driven tools can reach underserved areas, delivering educational content where traditional methods fall short. Moreover, AI addresses the digital divide by offering resources accessible to all students, regardless of geographic or economic background. By democratizing education, AI ensures that every child has the opportunity to learn, leveling the playing field and fostering a more equitable society. This shift benefits individual learners and communities, as education becomes a catalyst for social mobility and economic development.

Yet, with these advancements come ethical considerations that must be addressed. One significant concern is student data privacy in AI-driven learning platforms. As these systems collect and analyze vast amounts of personal data, safeguarding this information is paramount. Institutions must implement robust privacy measures to protect students' identities and ensure ethical use of their data. Moreover, the balance between AI assistance and human teaching is delicate. While AI can enhance learning, it should complement—not replace—the human element so vital in education. Teachers are not just conveyors of information but mentors and role models, providing emotional support and critical thinking skills that AI cannot replicate. Striking this balance is crucial to maintaining the integrity and effectiveness of educational systems.

To truly understand AI's impact in education, we must assess its social implications through comprehensive frameworks. Metrics for measuring educational outcomes provide valuable insights into how AI interventions affect learning. These assessments consider not only academic performance but also student engagement, creativity, and critical thinking skills. By evaluating these factors, educators can refine AI tools to better serve students' needs. Case studies of AI interventions in education systems offer practical examples of success and areas for improvement. For instance, some schools have implemented AI-driven programs that significantly boost literacy rates among students with learning disabilities, illustrating the potential of technology to transform lives.

In this dynamic landscape, AI stands as a powerful ally in shaping the future of education. It offers tools that adapt to individual needs, promotes equity by reaching the underserved, and enhances educational experiences while respecting ethical boundaries. However, the journey is ongoing, requiring continuous reflection and adaptation to ensure AI serves as a force for good in education. As we explore its possibilities, we are reminded of the responsibility to guide its development carefully, ensuring that technology enriches, rather than diminishes, the human experience of learning.

Policy and Governance in a Mindful AI Era

Imagine a bustling city where autonomous vehicles glide seamlessly alongside cyclists and pedestrians, managed by a sophisticated AI system that anticipates and mitigates congestion and accidents. This vision of urban harmony illustrates the profound impact of mindful AI governance. At its core, AI governance must be guided by principles that prioritize inclusivity and representation. Every voice, from technologists to everyday citizens, must have a say in how AI is developed and deployed. Inclusivity ensures that policies reflect the diverse needs of all communities, preventing any group from monopolizing AI advancements. Transparency and accountability are also cornerstones of AI governance. When regulatory processes are clear and open, they foster trust among stakeholders. People need to see how AI decisions are made and who is responsible for them, ensuring that systems remain aligned with societal values and ethical standards.

In crafting effective AI policies, stakeholder engagement is crucial. Bringing together a diverse group of voices ensures that policies are well-rounded and considerate of various perspectives. This collaborative approach not only enriches policy formulation but also enhances the legitimacy and acceptance of resulting regulations. Balancing innovation with regulation is another vital aspect. While rules are necessary to safeguard public interests, they must not stifle creativity and technological progress. Encouraging innovation while maintaining ethical oversight is a delicate act that requires thoughtful consideration and dynamic policies that can adapt as technology evolves.

Establishing global governance frameworks presents its own set of challenges. AI operates across borders, making it crucial to address cross-border data flows and jurisdictional issues. Without a cohesive framework, data privacy and security can vary dramatically from region to region, potentially leading to conflicts and gaps in protection. Harmonizing international AI ethical standards is essential to creating a unified approach to AI governance. This requires collaboration between nations, organizations, and industries to develop standards that transcend cultural and political differences, ensuring AI serves the global good.

Several case studies highlight successful AI governance initiatives. National AI strategies, such as those in Canada and Singapore, focus on promoting ethical development and deployment. These strategies emphasize the importance of ethical considerations in AI projects, ensuring technological advancements align with public values. International collaborations, like those led by the European Union, aim to establish common research and standards, facilitating cohesive AI governance across member states. Such collaborations demonstrate the power of collective effort in addressing AI's complex challenges.

As we navigate an era where AI increasingly influences our lives, mindful governance becomes more critical than ever. By embedding principles of inclusivity, transparency, and collaboration into AI policies, we can create systems that not only advance technological innovation but also uphold the values that define us as a society. In this landscape, the role of policymakers, technologists, and the public is to work together, ensuring that AI remains a force for good, enhancing the well-being of individuals and communities worldwide.

The Role of Psychologists in AI Development

In the vibrant field of AI development, psychologists contribute uniquely by bringing a deep understanding of human behavior. Their insights are crucial for designing AI systems that resonate with users on a fundamental level. Consider user behavior analysis: by examining how people interact with technology, psychologists help developers create AI systems that are intuitive and user-friendly. For instance, they might analyze how users navigate an app, identifying friction points that could be smoothed out. This ensures AI designs prioritize user needs, leading to a seamless experience that feels natural.

Moreover, psychologists offer insights into human-AI interaction patterns that are invaluable for developers. By understanding how users engage with AI, psychologists help create systems that feel more like partners than tools. This might involve designing AI that can pick up on subtle cues, such as hesitations or preferences, and adjust its responses accordingly. These insights are particularly important as AI systems become more integrated into daily life, requiring a nuanced understanding of human behavior to enhance user interaction.

Tackling bias and fairness in AI is another area where psychologists make a significant impact. AI systems often reflect the biases in their training data, leading to unfair outcomes. Psychologists can help identify these biases by applying their understanding of cognitive biases and social dynamics. They can collaborate with developers to create algorithms that are more inclusive and fair, reducing the risk of perpetuating existing inequalities. By addressing bias from a psychological perspective, AI systems can be designed to better serve diverse populations, ensuring fairness and equity in their applications.

Psychologists also play a pivotal role in enhancing AI user interface design. Drawing on psychological research, they guide usability testing to ensure interfaces are accessible and effective. They may conduct studies to assess how different design elements impact user experience, leading to interfaces that are both functional and enjoyable. Cognitive ergonomics—the study of how people interact with machines—focuses on reducing mental strain and improving efficiency. By applying these principles, psychologists help create AI systems that are not only powerful but also user-friendly.

Education and training are crucial for integrating psychological principles into AI development. Psychologists can lead workshops and training sessions for AI developers, sharing insights into human behavior and cognitive processes. These sessions equip developers with tools to consider psychological factors in their designs, leading to more empathetic and effective AI systems. Interdisciplinary courses that bridge psychology and technology provide a structured approach to understanding how these fields intersect. Through these educational efforts, developers gain a richer perspective on the human elements of AI, resulting in more thoughtful and humane systems.

Incorporating psychologists' expertise into AI development enriches the technology, making it more attuned to human needs and behaviors. As AI continues to evolve, the collaboration between psychologists and technologists will be crucial. This partnership not only enhances the functionality of AI systems but also ensures they are developed with empathy and fairness at their core. The insights psychologists bring help create AI that truly serves humanity, reflecting our values and aspirations. As we look to the future, this interdisciplinary collaboration will be key to navigating the ethical and practical challenges ahead.

CHAPTER 8
Practical Skills for AI Beginners

"Mindfulness invites us to be aware of how we affect the world. Similarly, AI should be developed with a focus on understanding its impact and making positive contributions."

Picture a bustling café filled with the hum of conversations and the tapping of keyboards. Amidst the clatter of coffee cups, a young student sits with a laptop open to a web of AI terminology, trying to make sense of the complex jargon filling the screen. Whether you're a technologist, an ethicist, a psychologist, an educator, or a policymaker, you've likely encountered similar moments of bewilderment when venturing into the world of artificial intelligence. This chapter aims to demystify AI jargon, transforming those moments of confusion into clarity and confidence. By breaking down complex terms into simple, understandable language and providing relatable examples, we'll make AI accessible to you, regardless of your background or expertise.

Let's start with the basics: an algorithm is a set of rules a machine follows to perform tasks, akin to a recipe guiding the preparation of your favorite dish. Algorithms are the foundation of AI, enabling machines to execute complex operations efficiently. Now, consider neural networks—intricate systems inspired by the human brain's architecture, designed to recognize patterns and learn from data. Imagine a network of interconnected pathways, each node processing information and passing it along, much like neurons firing in our brains. This setup allows AI to make sense of vast datasets, identifying trends and anomalies with remarkable precision.

Machine learning is the process by which these algorithms enable machines to learn and adapt without explicit programming, much like a child learning to read by recognizing letters and words. Within this realm, supervised learning involves teaching machines using labeled datasets, where each input has a corresponding output, like a teacher guiding a student through a math problem with step-by-step instructions. Unsupervised learning, on the other hand, allows algorithms to infer patterns from unlabeled data, much like a detective piecing together clues to solve a mystery without a clear solution in sight.

To illustrate these concepts, consider social media analytics as an example of "big data" in action. Every post, like, and comment contributes to an immense dataset that AI systems analyze to uncover user behavior patterns. This analysis informs targeted advertisements and content recommendations, tailoring your online experience. Conversely, natural language processing (NLP) enables voice-activated assistants to understand and respond to spoken commands. Through NLP, machines interpret human language, transforming your verbal requests into actionable tasks, whether setting a reminder or playing your favorite song.

Visual aids like flowcharts can enhance your understanding of these processes. Picture a flowchart depicting machine learning steps: data collection, data preprocessing, model training, and evaluation. Each step, outlined visually, provides a roadmap of the journey from raw data to actionable insights. Infographics further illustrate AI's impact across various industries, from healthcare to finance, by showcasing how these technologies streamline operations and drive innovation.

To support your exploration of AI, I've included a comprehensive glossary of terms. This resource offers an alphabetical listing of AI phrases, complete with brief descriptions and practical examples. For instance, you'll find clear definitions of terms like "autonomous," which refers to machines performing tasks without human intervention, or "cognitive computing," a term often used to describe AI systems that simulate human thought processes.

As you immerse yourself in this chapter, remember that understanding AI is not about mastering every technical detail but rather developing a foundational grasp of key concepts. Whether you're developing AI policies, designing ethical AI systems, or exploring the psychological impacts of AI, these practical skills will empower you to engage with AI confidently and thoughtfully. Embrace this opportunity to expand your knowledge and contribute to the evolving landscape of artificial intelligence.

8.2 Hands-On AI: Projects and Exercises for Beginners

Imagine you're sitting at your desk, computer open, ready to dive into the world of AI through hands-on projects. The idea of creating something tangible with AI might seem daunting, but it's surprisingly accessible. Let's start with a simple yet rewarding project: building a basic chatbot. Using open-source tools like Python's ChatterBot library, you can construct a chatbot that engages in simple conversations. Begin by setting up your environment—installing Python and the necessary libraries. Once that's done, you'll write a script that allows your chatbot to greet users and respond to basic queries. As you code, you'll learn to train your bot with data, enabling it to improve its interactions over time. This exercise not only familiarizes you with fundamental coding principles but also demonstrates how AI can be applied in everyday contexts.

Another exciting project involves creating an image classifier using available datasets, such as the popular MNIST dataset of handwritten digits. This task will introduce you to machine learning concepts, where you'll train a model to recognize and categorize images. Start by downloading the dataset and setting up a Jupyter Notebook, which is widely used for data science projects. Your first task is to preprocess the data, ensuring it's ready for the model to analyze. Next, you'll design a neural network—a series of algorithms that mimic human brain function—and train it using your dataset. As the model learns, it will improve its accuracy in identifying images, providing a gratifying sense of accomplishment as you watch your AI become more adept.

To ensure your projects succeed, I'll guide you through each step with detailed instructions. Begin by writing and testing code snippets, breaking down complex problems into manageable tasks. As you write code, you'll encounter errors—these are not setbacks but opportunities to learn. Debugging is an essential skill in programming, allowing you to identify and fix issues that arise. Use tools like Python's debugger or online forums to troubleshoot common errors. As you refine your code, you'll gain a deeper understanding of AI's inner workings, boosting your confidence and technical skills.

Experimentation is the heart of learning in AI. Once your basic projects are functional, challenge yourself by modifying existing AI models to test new outcomes. Change parameters, add new data inputs, or experiment with different algorithms to see how they affect performance. This hands-on approach fosters a mindset of curiosity and discovery, encouraging you to explore the vast possibilities AI offers. Experiment with various datasets to gain diverse insights. Whether you're analyzing social media trends or climate data, each dataset presents unique challenges that enhance your analytical abilities.

As you engage with these projects, take time to reflect on your experiences. Document the challenges you face and the solutions you devise. This practice not only solidifies your understanding but also creates a valuable resource for future reference. Share your project results with peers, seeking feedback and collaboration. Engaging with a community of learners enriches your journey, offering fresh perspectives and support. By reflecting and sharing, you cultivate a growth mindset, essential for continual learning and improvement in the ever-evolving field of AI.

8.3 Developing a Mindful AI Literacy Curriculum

Imagine walking into a classroom buzzing with excitement, where students eagerly engage with AI concepts that are seamlessly integrated into their learning journey. Creating an effective AI curriculum starts with aligning content to meet learners' needs and goals. This means understanding the diverse backgrounds of students—be they technologists, ethicists, psychologists, or policymakers—and crafting lessons that resonate with their unique perspectives. Begin by incorporating ethical discussions into your lessons, prompting students to consider the impact of AI on society, privacy, and human values. These discussions not only deepen their understanding but also cultivate critical thinking skills, empowering them to make informed decisions in their future careers.

To captivate students, consider developing interactive modules that bring AI concepts to life. Gamified learning experiences can transform abstract ideas into tangible challenges, engaging students in a playful yet educational manner. Imagine a simulation where students design their own AI algorithms to solve real-world problems, competing against each other to optimize their solutions. Virtual labs offer another avenue for hands-on experimentation, allowing learners to apply theoretical knowledge in a controlled environment. These labs can simulate scenarios like training a neural network to recognize patterns or fine-tuning an AI model for specific tasks. By fostering an interactive learning environment, you encourage exploration and creativity, making AI education both enjoyable and impactful.

Assessment and evaluation are crucial components of any curriculum, providing insights into learners' progress and understanding. Design quizzes and practical assessments that test not only factual knowledge but also the application of AI concepts. For instance, challenge students to develop a simple AI project, evaluating their ability to integrate technical skills with ethical considerations. Peer reviews and group discussions can enrich the learning experience, offering diverse perspectives and fostering collaboration. Encourage students to present their projects and engage in constructive feedback sessions, where they learn from each other's successes and challenges. This collaborative approach nurtures a supportive learning community, where students grow together and share their insights.

Compiling a comprehensive resource list supports both educators and learners, offering a wealth of materials to explore beyond the classroom. Begin with recommended readings and online courses that cover a broad spectrum of AI topics. These resources should cater to various learning preferences, from in-depth academic texts to engaging multimedia content. Consider including tools and platforms that facilitate AI education, such as coding environments and data visualization software. These resources empower educators to tailor their teaching methods and provide learners with opportunities to delve deeper into specific areas of interest. By equipping students with a diverse array of resources, you inspire continuous learning and curiosity, encouraging them to stay informed and engaged in the ever-evolving world of AI.

8.4 Using AI Tools in Everyday Life

Imagine starting your day with an AI-powered app that organizes your schedule, sends gentle reminders for meetings, and even suggests the fastest route to work. These productivity apps are more than just digital assistants; they're becoming integral to our daily routines. From managing your calendar to optimizing your workflow, AI tools like Notion AI or Trello are designed to streamline tasks and increase efficiency. These applications analyze your habits and tasks, offering suggestions to help you prioritize effectively.

Personal finance management is another area where AI tools shine. Imagine an app that not only tracks your spending but also analyzes your financial patterns, offering insights and recommendations for saving and investing. Tools like Mint and PocketGuard provide a comprehensive view of your financial landscape, helping you make informed decisions effortlessly.

In the realm of smart home devices, AI capabilities are revolutionizing how we interact with our living spaces. Picture a home where lights adjust automatically based on the time of day, thermostats learn your preferred temperatures, and security systems adapt to your schedule. Devices like Google Nest and Amazon Echo serve as central hubs that integrate various aspects of home management, making daily tasks more convenient. These tools don't just respond to commands; they learn from your routines, creating an intuitive environment that anticipates your needs. The seamless integration of AI into home management is not only about convenience but also about enhancing your quality of life by reducing the mental load of managing your home.

Incorporating AI tools into your routine can be as simple as automating scheduling and reminders. AI assistants like Siri, Google Assistant, or Alexa help you manage your time by setting alarms, scheduling meetings, and reminding you of important tasks. Consider meal planning and grocery shopping—AI can suggest recipes based on your dietary preferences and even create shopping lists, ensuring you never miss an ingredient. Apps like Yummly and AnyList integrate AI to personalize meal plans and simplify grocery shopping, making healthy eating habits easier to maintain. By leveraging AI for these everyday tasks, you free up mental space, allowing you to focus on what truly matters.

When evaluating the effectiveness of AI tools, consider factors like user reviews and ratings, which provide insights into real-world performance and user satisfaction. Compare features across different tools to determine which best meets your needs, and conduct a cost-benefit analysis to assess the value offered by each app. This evaluation process ensures that you choose tools that enhance your productivity without unnecessary complexity. It's essential to select tools that not only meet functional requirements but also align with your personal workflow and preferences. The right AI tools should feel intuitive, seamlessly integrating into your life without requiring significant adjustments to your daily habits.

Staying updated on new AI tools and advancements can seem daunting, but it doesn't have to be. Subscribing to tech newsletters and blogs like *TechCrunch* or *The Verge* keeps you informed about the latest innovations and trends. These resources offer reviews, comparisons, and insights into emerging technologies, helping you make informed decisions about which tools to adopt. Participating in online AI forums and communities provides a platform for sharing experiences and learning from others. Engaging with a community of like-minded individuals fosters knowledge exchange and offers support as you navigate the ever-evolving landscape of AI tools. This proactive approach ensures that you remain at the forefront of technology, ready to capitalize on new opportunities as they arise.

8.5 Evaluating AI Resources and Further Learning

As you navigate the vast landscape of AI, it's crucial to hone your critical evaluation skills. These skills will enable you to sift through the abundance of information and discern what is credible and valuable. Start by identifying trustworthy sources and authors. Look for publications from established research institutions, reputable universities, or well-known experts in the field. Check the credentials of authors to ensure they have the expertise necessary to discuss AI topics accurately. A reliable source often includes citations and references to peer-reviewed studies, adding weight to the information presented.

Analyzing the depth and accuracy of information is equally important. Consider whether the resource provides a balanced view, acknowledging different perspectives and potential limitations. This well-rounded approach not only enhances your understanding but also enables you to apply AI concepts more effectively.

To support your learning journey, consider curated learning paths that offer structure and direction. Whether you're a beginner or an advanced learner, there are courses and certifications designed to meet your needs. Platforms like Coursera, edX, and Udacity offer a range of AI-related courses that cater to different skill levels and interests. Start with foundational courses that introduce key concepts and gradually progress to more specialized topics, such as deep learning or AI ethics.

In addition to formal courses, explore suggested reading lists tailored to your interests. These lists might include books that delve into AI's impact on society, cutting-edge research papers, or articles that explore the intersections of AI with various fields. By following a structured learning path, you can build a comprehensive understanding of AI while continuously challenging yourself to expand your knowledge.

Community engagement plays a pivotal role in enhancing your AI learning experience. Joining AI communities allows you to collaborate with others, exchange ideas, and stay motivated. Online forums, such as Reddit's Machine Learning community or Stack Exchange's AI section, provide platforms for asking questions, sharing insights, and learning from diverse perspectives. Participate in discussions and contribute your knowledge to help others.

Local AI meetups and workshops offer opportunities for face-to-face interactions with fellow enthusiasts and professionals. These events often feature guest speakers, hands-on activities, and networking sessions, creating a dynamic learning environment. By engaging with the AI community, you not only reinforce your learning but also build valuable connections that can support your growth in the field.

Staying informed about AI trends is essential in a rapidly evolving field. Follow AI thought leaders on social media platforms like Twitter or LinkedIn, where they share insights, news, and updates about the latest developments. Thought leaders often provide unique perspectives and highlight emerging technologies that might not yet be widely covered.

Attending AI webinars and conferences is another effective way to keep up with advancements. Events such as the Neural Information Processing Systems (NeurIPS) conference or the International Conference on Machine Learning (ICML) showcase groundbreaking research and innovations. These gatherings offer a chance to hear from experts, participate in discussions, and gain firsthand exposure to cutting-edge technologies.

Staying informed not only enhances your knowledge but also positions you to anticipate future trends and opportunities in AI, enabling you to make informed decisions and contribute meaningfully to the field.

CHAPTER 9

Addressing Common Concerns and Objections

"Mindfulness in AI development means taking the time to think about not just the 'how' but the 'why'—why does AI exist, and how can it serve the well-being of all?"

Picture this: you're at a bustling tech conference, surrounded by experts passionately discussing the latest AI innovations. Yet, as you listen, the buzzwords fly over your head, and the jargon becomes a barrier rather than a bridge. This scenario is all too familiar for many who encounter the world of AI. The language of AI can seem daunting, filled with terms that sound like a foreign dialect. However, breaking down these terms into relatable language can transform confusion into clarity, making AI accessible to everyone, regardless of their background.

Demystifying technical language begins with simplifying complex jargon. Consider machine learning, a foundational concept in AI. At its core, machine learning is akin to teaching a child to recognize objects. Just as a child learns to identify a cat by seeing various pictures, an AI system learns to recognize patterns by analyzing data. This analogy helps transform an abstract concept into something tangible and relatable. Similarly, neural networks, which are critical to AI's function, can be compared to the structure of the human brain. They mimic the way neurons connect and process information, enabling AI to perform tasks like image recognition and language processing. By comparing these processes to everyday tasks, we can illuminate how AI functions in a more familiar context.

Providing context is essential for making technical language accessible. AI's terminology is rooted in practical applications, often connected to technology we use daily. For instance, when we talk about "natural language processing" (NLP), we're referring to the ability of AI to understand and generate human language. This capability powers chatbots that handle customer inquiries or voice assistants that respond to our commands. By linking AI terms to their applications, we can create a bridge between abstract concepts and real-world usage. This approach not only demystifies the language of AI but also highlights its relevance in our lives, making it easier for you to grasp and apply these concepts in your work or studies.

To further aid your understanding, a comprehensive glossary can serve as an invaluable resource. An alphabetized list of AI terms with simple definitions provides a quick reference guide, allowing you to familiarize yourself with key terminology at your own pace. Highlighting frequently used terms in AI discussions ensures you have a solid foundation to engage in conversations and explore AI literature confidently. This glossary acts as a tool for empowerment, enabling you to navigate the complexities of AI language with ease. By having a reliable reference at your fingertips, you can build your knowledge incrementally, reinforcing your comprehension of AI's many facets.

Interactive learning tools offer dynamic ways to engage with AI terminology. Online glossaries featuring multimedia explanations can enrich your learning experience by providing visual and auditory aids to complement textual definitions. These resources cater to diverse learning styles, ensuring that you can absorb information in a way that resonates with you. Additionally, apps that provide daily AI term definitions can keep you informed and engaged, gradually building your vocabulary over time. Such tools transform learning from a passive activity into an interactive journey, fostering deeper understanding and retention of AI concepts. By incorporating these tools into your routine, you can develop a nuanced grasp of AI language, enhancing your ability to communicate and collaborate effectively in the field.

Interactive Exercise: Building Your AI Vocabulary

Spend a few minutes each day exploring a new AI term from an online glossary or app. Note its definition and reflect on how it applies to your field or interests. Discuss these terms with colleagues or peers to deepen your understanding through conversation. This practice will help you engage with AI topics confidently, breaking down barriers and fostering meaningful dialogue.

9.2 Ensuring Relevance: Keeping AI Knowledge Current

In the ever-evolving landscape of artificial intelligence, keeping your knowledge up to date isn't a luxury—it's a necessity. As AI advances, staying informed requires a proactive, dynamic approach. Regularly engaging with AI-focused publications and blogs is an effective way to keep up. These sources provide insights into the latest trends, breakthroughs, and industry applications, ensuring you stay ahead. Whether it's an analysis of a new AI model or a discussion on ethical implications, these resources bridge the gap between you and cutting-edge developments. Additionally, participating in webinars and online courses broadens your understanding and introduces emerging concepts. These digital platforms let you learn from global experts in a flexible, interactive format, removing barriers of geography and time.

Identifying credible sources is crucial when navigating the vast sea of AI information. In a world where content is abundant but not always reliable, assessing quality is key. Start by checking the author's credentials—reputable experts bring depth and credibility to their analyses. Consider the publication's reputation, as established outlets maintain higher editorial standards. Timeliness matters, too, since AI evolves rapidly, making outdated insights less relevant. Ensure the information aligns with current developments and practical applications. By refining your ability to filter content, you can focus on valuable insights rather than noise.

Building connections with AI professionals provides another advantage. Networking is a powerful tool for staying informed. Joining AI-focused forums and professional groups allows you to engage with thought leaders and peers who share your interests. These platforms foster idea exchanges, collaborations, and discussions that shape the future of AI. Attending conferences offers further benefits, giving you direct access to experts and diverse perspectives on complex topics. Engaging in these communities strengthens your understanding and keeps you connected to ongoing advancements.

Leveraging technology to receive AI updates makes staying informed easier. Setting up news alerts ensures the latest developments come directly to you, eliminating the need to search manually. Tailor these alerts to focus on specific areas of interest, such as ethical AI, machine learning innovations, or industry-specific applications. Using RSS feeds to aggregate AI news from multiple sources creates a centralized hub for updates, saving time and providing a comprehensive view of trends. By integrating these tools into your routine, you ensure a steady flow of relevant information, keeping you prepared for AI's rapid evolution.

Resource List: Recommended AI Publications and Blogs

Subscribe to leading AI publications like *Wired*, *MIT Technology Review*, and *AI Magazine* for in-depth analyses and insights. Explore blogs such as *Towards Data Science* and *Analytics Vidhya* for practical tutorials and community discussions. These resources offer a balanced mix of theory and application, helping you stay informed and deepen your understanding.

9.3 Comprehensive Ethical Explorations: Going Beyond the Surface

Imagine AI systems that not only track your actions but also understand your location and emotions. This reality underscores the need for strong ethical principles, as AI increasingly affects privacy and autonomy. The implications for privacy are significant—AI can collect and analyze vast amounts of personal data, making safeguards essential to protect individual rights. Autonomy is also at risk, as AI can subtly influence decisions without users even realizing it. Case studies highlight these ethical dilemmas. For instance, an AI hiring model that unintentionally favors certain demographics due to biased training data demonstrates the need for transparency and fairness. Examining such cases deepens your understanding of AI's ethical challenges and prepares you to address them effectively.

Engaging in ethical debates is crucial for shaping AI's future. Academic journals and conferences provide platforms for experts to discuss AI ethics, offering insights into responsible deployment. By participating in these discussions, you can contribute your perspective while learning from others. Community discussions are equally valuable, allowing diverse voices to explore ethical concerns and propose solutions. These conversations are not just theoretical—they influence policy development and AI design. By immersing yourself in these debates, you actively contribute to AI's ethical evolution, helping steer it toward responsible and fair use.

Developing your own ethical framework empowers you to navigate AI's complexities. Reflect on your values and how they shape your views on fairness, privacy, and societal impact. Creating a checklist of ethical considerations—such as data privacy, bias detection, and user consent—can be a practical tool for evaluating AI systems. Regularly revisiting and refining your ethical stance ensures it remains relevant as AI evolves. This practice not only informs your engagement with AI but also strengthens your ability to advocate for ethical standards in your work and community.

Integrating ethics into AI practice requires deliberate strategies and collaboration. Establishing clear ethical guidelines for projects sets a foundation for accountability and responsible decision-making. These guidelines should be specific, actionable, and address potential ethical risks. Collaboration with ethicists enhances this process, bringing expertise to identify and resolve ethical concerns early in development. By embedding ethical considerations throughout AI projects, you foster a culture of responsibility and transparency. Prioritizing ethics ensures that AI systems are not just innovative but also aligned with societal values, contributing to the common good.

9.4 Tailoring AI Insights to Your Field

Understanding how AI transforms specific industries is essential in leveraging its full potential. Take healthcare, for example. AI has revolutionized diagnostics, enabling faster, more accurate disease detection through imaging technologies that surpass human capabilities. It has also streamlined administrative tasks, allowing healthcare professionals to focus more on patient care. In finance, AI powers sophisticated algorithms that predict market trends and detect fraud with remarkable precision. This enhances decision-making while strengthening security measures that protect consumer assets. Meanwhile, agriculture benefits from AI-driven precision farming, which optimizes crop yields, reduces water usage, and minimizes environmental impact. Exploring AI's unique applications across sectors reveals how traditional practices can evolve into cutting-edge solutions that address industry-specific challenges.

To tailor AI resources to your field, curate learning materials that align with your sector's needs. If you work in finance, focus on algorithmic trading and risk assessment models, which offer practical insights beyond foundational AI concepts. In healthcare, explore case studies on AI-driven patient monitoring and personalized medicine. These examples illustrate AI's transformative potential and inspire real-world applications. Creating an industry-specific reading list helps you stay informed about the latest trends, ensuring your knowledge remains relevant and impactful.

Collaborative learning opportunities further expand your understanding of AI applications. Forming study groups with peers from different disciplines fosters an environment where diverse perspectives converge to solve complex problems. Cross-industry workshops and seminars enhance this experience, providing platforms for idea exchange and adaptation of AI across contexts. For instance, a workshop that unites professionals from healthcare, agriculture, and finance can generate innovative AI-driven solutions that span multiple sectors. This collaborative approach not only broadens your knowledge but also builds a network of professionals dedicated to advancing AI in their respective fields.

Assessing AI's benefits and challenges in specific sectors requires a thoughtful cost-benefit analysis. In healthcare, AI technologies may demand significant upfront investment, but long-term benefits—such as improved patient outcomes and operational efficiencies—often justify the cost. Similarly, in agriculture, AI-driven precision farming can reduce resource waste and increase yields. However, ethical concerns must also be considered. In finance, for example, AI-powered loan approvals must be scrutinized for fairness and bias. Evaluating these factors ensures AI adoption aligns with both economic and ethical considerations.

AI's potential to revolutionize industries is immense, but success depends on a nuanced approach that considers unique challenges and opportunities. By tailoring AI insights to your sector, collaborating with diverse professionals, and carefully assessing its benefits and risks, you can harness AI to drive meaningful change. This strategic approach not only enhances your expertise but also positions you at the forefront of innovation, enabling you to contribute effectively to AI's evolution in your industry.

9.5 Overcoming Skepticism: Building Trust in AI Resources

When discussing AI, skepticism often arises from misconceptions. One common myth is that AI will replace human jobs entirely. While AI automates certain tasks, it is not a universal substitute for human capabilities. Instead, it handles repetitive, mundane work, allowing people to focus on more complex, creative, and strategic roles. This shift requires adaptation but does not spell the end of employment. Understanding AI's strengths and limitations is crucial. AI excels at processing vast data sets and recognizing patterns but struggles with emotional intelligence, nuanced judgment, and contextual understanding. Clarifying these misconceptions reduces fear and promotes a balanced perspective on AI's role in the workforce.

Education plays a key role in overcoming skepticism. Short courses and workshops on AI fundamentals empower individuals with the knowledge to engage confidently with AI technologies. These programs break down complex concepts into manageable, relatable topics. Certification programs further validate AI expertise, providing a structured path for learners to demonstrate their understanding. This approach builds confidence and equips individuals with the skills to navigate AI's evolving landscape. As more people gain AI literacy, they become better equipped to evaluate and integrate AI solutions in their personal and professional lives.

Showcasing successful AI implementations can also dismantle skepticism. In healthcare, AI enhances diagnostic accuracy and personalizes treatment plans, improving patient outcomes. In education, AI-driven systems adapt to individual student needs, creating more effective learning environments. These examples highlight AI's positive contributions, demonstrating its potential to enhance rather than replace human capabilities. By documenting real-world successes, we shift the narrative toward AI as a valuable tool that supports human progress.

Engaging with trusted AI communities further builds confidence in AI's potential. These communities provide spaces for individuals to exchange ideas, share experiences, and learn from experts. Forums moderated by AI specialists offer access to reliable information and thoughtful discussions. Community events focused on ethical AI use foster deeper engagement and collaboration. These interactions create a sense of belonging and shared purpose, encouraging informed and responsible AI adoption. By joining these communities, individuals can stay updated, connect with like-minded peers, and contribute to shaping AI's ethical development.

As Chapter 9 concludes, overcoming skepticism and building trust in AI requires a multifaceted approach. Addressing misconceptions, expanding education, highlighting success stories, and fostering community engagement lay the groundwork for a more informed and confident approach to AI. Moving forward, the next chapter will explore the practical skills needed to work with AI effectively, equipping you to navigate this rapidly evolving field with insight and adaptability.

CHAPTER 10
Innovative Learning Pathways and Community Engagement

"Mindfulness is the art of understanding what is happening right now—AI can reflect this principle by continuously learning and adjusting based on real-time data and ethical considerations."

In a vibrant classroom, students aren't just staring at textbooks. Instead, they're immersed in a digital environment where an AI platform adapts lessons to each student's unique pace and style. This isn't a distant dream—it's a reality shaped by the convergence of AI and education. Imagine a space filled with the hum of curiosity, where students explore complex concepts through interactive simulations, guided by AI systems that learn alongside them. The potential for AI to transform education is immense, fostering not just knowledge but also a sense of wonder and engagement in learners of all ages.

Creating Interactive Learning Experiences with AI

The potential of AI in crafting interactive learning experiences is vast. Engaging AI-driven learning platforms have revolutionized how we approach education. These platforms harness the power of adaptive learning systems, tailoring content to match each learner's pace and style. Imagine a student struggling with algebra concepts—an AI system identifies these challenges and adjusts the curriculum, providing additional resources and exercises until mastery is achieved. This personalization extends beyond academics, offering students tailored pathways aligned with their interests and career aspirations.

Gamified AI modules further enhance engagement by introducing elements of play and competition into learning. These modules transform mundane tasks into exciting challenges, motivating students to participate actively and achieve their goals. By integrating adaptive learning systems and gamified elements, educational experiences become dynamic and student-centered, fostering a love of learning that extends beyond the classroom.

Virtual reality (VR) complements AI by creating immersive educational environments that captivate and inspire. With VR, students can embark on virtual field trips, exploring historical sites, distant planets, or even the inner workings of the human body—all from the safety of their classroom. These experiences offer a level of immersion and interactivity that traditional methods cannot match.

Virtual labs allow students to experiment with AI models, providing hands-on experience in a risk-free setting. Imagine a biology student dissecting a virtual frog, exploring its anatomy without ethical concerns or logistical challenges. Similarly, simulated scenarios enable students to apply theoretical knowledge to real-world applications, reinforcing learning through practice. This blend of VR and AI not only enhances understanding but also sparks creativity and curiosity, encouraging students to explore and experiment in ways previously unimaginable.

Interactive workshops and webinars powered by AI technology bring a new dimension to learning. These sessions facilitate real-time engagement, allowing participants to interact with experts and peers in a dynamic, collaborative environment. Live coding sessions, for instance, enable learners to see the immediate impact of their work, with AI systems providing instant feedback and suggestions. This fosters a sense of accomplishment and accelerates the learning process.

AI-assisted Q&A forums also play a crucial role, offering real-time problem-solving opportunities. Students can pose questions and receive tailored responses from AI systems, which analyze queries and provide relevant information from vast datasets. This approach enhances understanding and encourages active participation, empowering students to explore topics in depth.

AI-based assessment tools represent a paradigm shift in evaluating learner progress. Automated grading systems provide timely, personalized feedback, helping students understand their strengths and weaknesses without delay. These systems analyze patterns in performance, identifying areas for improvement and suggesting targeted resources. For educators, this technology offers valuable insights for tracking learning outcomes and adjusting instruction to meet diverse needs.

By leveraging AI in assessments, educators can move beyond traditional testing, embracing a holistic approach that prioritizes growth over rote memorization. This shift not only improves educational outcomes but also reduces stress, as students receive constructive feedback tailored to their individual needs.

Reflection Section: Enhancing Learning with AI

Consider the potential of AI to transform your field. Reflect on how adaptive learning systems and immersive technologies could enhance educational experiences. What challenges might arise in implementing these tools, and how could they be addressed to ensure equitable access? Write down your thoughts, considering the broader implications for learners and educators alike.

As we explore these innovative learning pathways, it's clear that integrating AI into education holds immense promise. By creating interactive, personalized, and immersive experiences, we can unlock new possibilities for learning and growth. This chapter invites you to envision a future where education is not confined to the walls of a classroom but is a dynamic, evolving journey shaped by the needs and aspirations of each learner.

Insights from AI Experts: Interviews and Perspectives

In the ever-evolving landscape of artificial intelligence, expert voices provide guidance. Engaging with those at the frontier of AI offers invaluable insights into its future. I had the privilege of speaking with leaders across various sectors, each bringing a unique perspective. These conversations revealed not only the technological advancements on the horizon but also the ethical considerations that must accompany progress.

One prominent AI researcher shared his vision of AI systems that do more than assist—they become integral partners in creativity and problem-solving. He predicted that in the next decade, AI would seamlessly integrate into workflows, enhancing human capabilities in unprecedented ways. Yet, he emphasized that with this power comes responsibility. Ensuring AI systems are developed with fairness and transparency is crucial to fostering trust and acceptance. His insights echoed a common refrain among experts: the need to balance innovation with ethics.

Ethicists added another layer to these discussions, offering a lens through which to view AI's societal impact. One renowned ethicist described the delicate balance between technological advancement and moral responsibility. She highlighted the need for robust frameworks to guide AI development, preventing systems from perpetuating existing biases. Her work focuses on creating adaptable ethical guidelines, ensuring relevance in a world where technology evolves faster than regulations.

Psychologists examined AI's impact on human behavior. One researcher noted that while AI offers convenience, it also raises questions about autonomy. Her studies explore how reliance on technology might alter cognitive functions and interpersonal relationships. She stressed the importance of designing AI systems that augment rather than diminish human capabilities, fostering environments where technology supports human judgment.

Educators provided practical insights into integrating AI into curricula. One educator described AI's transformative potential for personalized learning, bridging gaps and fostering inclusivity. However, she also addressed challenges, such as ensuring equitable access to technology. Her insights underscored the dual role of educators as facilitators of learning and advocates for equity in the digital age.

Conversations with AI pioneers offered a glimpse into the past and future of the field. One pioneer shared a story of overcoming skepticism and technical hurdles in AI's early days. His perseverance laid the groundwork for many technologies we now take for granted. These stories highlight the resilience and creativity that drive AI development, reminding us of the untapped potential in technological advancement.

Exploring AI across disciplines revealed the collaborative nature of innovation. Technologists discussed advancements in AI hardware and neural networks, while policymakers emphasized the need for international cooperation. Through these interviews, a tapestry of insights emerges, weaving together AI's potential and challenges.

Building a Community of Mindful AI Practitioners

In an era where AI drives innovation, building a community of mindful AI practitioners is crucial. This community fosters shared learning, collaboration, and ethical development. Online forums and discussion groups provide platforms for exchanging ideas, addressing challenges, and celebrating achievements.

Local meetups and hackathons further enhance engagement, bringing people together for hands-on collaboration. These events encourage participants to brainstorm, code, and prototype new ideas, fostering a sense of camaraderie and shared purpose. Hackathons offer unique opportunities to test skills, gain feedback, and integrate ethical considerations into AI development.

Mentorship plays a key role in this community, connecting beginners with experienced practitioners. Mentors offer guidance, while mentees bring fresh perspectives, fostering a reciprocal learning experience. Regular newsletters, success stories, and incentives for contributions ensure sustained engagement.

By fostering an inclusive, engaged network of AI practitioners, we can create a culture of mindfulness that guides ethical innovation. As we turn to the next chapter, we explore how these principles can inform AI governance and policy-making.

Conclusion

As we conclude this exploration of mindfulness and AI, it's time to reflect on our journey. Throughout this book, we've examined how principles like awareness, compassion, and ethical judgment can be integrated into AI development. Our goal has been clear: to create AI systems that are not just functional but ethical and compassionate—systems that respect human values and enhance well-being.

Our vision for AI is ambitious yet achievable. We imagine a future where AI acts as a trusted partner, assisting in ethical decision-making and enriching our lives. Throughout these chapters, we've explored how a mindful approach to AI can transform healthcare, education, and policy. By focusing on intentional development, we ensure AI aligns with societal values and contributes positively to communities.

Key takeaways from this discussion are crucial. First, interdisciplinary collaboration is essential for integrating mindfulness into AI. Bringing together technologists, ethicists, psychologists, and policymakers fosters innovation while ensuring ethical considerations like fairness, transparency, and accountability. AI's impact—whether enhancing patient care or personalizing learning—underscores its potential for meaningful social change.

Looking ahead, mindfulness will be pivotal in shaping AI's evolution. As technology advances, embedding ethical principles will guide its development in ways that prioritize human values. This approach helps navigate AI's challenges and opportunities, ensuring it remains a force for good.

I encourage you to apply the insights from this book to your field. Whether you're a technologist, educator, or policymaker, your role in advocating for mindful AI is critical. Engage in discussions, participate in initiatives, and champion ethical AI development. Your contributions can shape a future where technology enhances rather than diminishes our humanity.

Continued learning is vital in this rapidly evolving landscape. Stay informed about AI trends through further reading and resources to remain at the forefront of innovation and ethical integration.

Community engagement is another powerful tool. Joining or forming groups focused on mindful AI fosters collaboration and the exchange of best practices. These spaces drive progress, ensuring collective knowledge leads to responsible innovation.

As we conclude, consider this: how will you contribute to a future where technology and mindfulness coexist harmoniously? The potential is vast, and the responsibility is shared. Together, we can shape a world where AI upholds our values, respects our humanity, and enhances our lives. Let's move forward with intention and purpose, ensuring technology serves as a true partner in building a better world.

References

- *Integrating Mindfulness in AI: A New Frontier for Ethical ...* https://www.dailyhuman.com/post/mindful-ai

- *The History of Artificial Intelligence: Complete AI Timeline* https://www.techtarget.com/searchenterpriseai/tip/The-history-of-artificial-intelligence-Complete-AI-timeline

- *A Unified Framework of Five Principles for AI in Society* https://hdsr.mitpress.mit.edu/pub/l0jsh9d1

- *AI In Mental Health: Opportunities And Challenges ...* https://www.forbes.com/sites/bernardmarr/2023/07/06/ai-in-mental-health-opportunities-and-challenges-in-developing-intelligent-digital-therapies/

- *Ethics guidelines for trustworthy AI* https://digital-strategy.ec.europa.eu/en/library/ethics-guidelines-trustworthy-ai

- *The IEEE Global Initiative 2.0 on Ethics of Autonomous and ...* https://standards.ieee.org/industry-connections/activities/ieee-global-initiative/

- *How AI Algorithmic Bias Affects Society | Fast Data Science* https://fastdatascience.com/ai-ethics/bias-in-ai-algorithmic-bias-society/

- *Survey on Explainable AI: Techniques, challenges and ...* https://www.sciencedirect.com/science/article/pii/S095741742401577X

- *How AI impacts the way people feel, think, and behave* https://www.sciencedirect.com/science/article/pii/S2352250X24000484
- *AI in Mental Health: A New Revolution in Diagnosis and ...* https://vinbrain.net/ai-in-mental-health-a-new-revolution-in-diagnosis-and-treatment
- *What is AI Bias? - Understanding Its Impact, Risks, and ...* https://www.holisticai.com/blog/what-is-ai-bias-risks-mitigation-strategies#:~:text=AI%20bias%20occurs%20when%20machine,hiring%2C%20lending%2C%20or%20healthcare.
- *Collaborative Intelligence: Humans and AI Are Joining ...* https://hbr.org/2018/07/collaborative-intelligence-humans-and-ai-are-joining-forces
- *Health Equity and Ethical Considerations in Using Artificial ...* https://www.cdc.gov/pcd/issues/2024/24_0245.htm
- *Using AI to Personalize Learning & Education* https://www.docebo.com/learning-network/blog/personalized-learning-ai/
- *Blueprint for an AI Bill of Rights | OSTP* https://www.whitehouse.gov/ostp/ai-bill-of-rights/
- *How artificial intelligence is helping tackle environmental ...* https://www.unep.org/news-and-stories/story/how-artificial-intelligence-helping-tackle-environmental-challenges

- *Concerns of an Artificial Intelligence Pioneer* https://www.quantamagazine.org/artificial-intelligence-aligned-with-human-values-qa-with-stuart-russell-20150421/

- *Integrating Mindfulness in AI: A New Frontier for Ethical ...* https://www.dailyhuman.com/post/mindful-ai

- *Delivery of Compassionate Mental Health Care in a Digital ...* https://pmc.ncbi.nlm.nih.gov/articles/PMC7084292/

- *Guidelines for Integrating Value Sensitive Design in ...* https://dl.acm.org/doi/10.1145/3613904.3642810

- *Integrating Mindfulness in AI: A New Frontier for Ethical ...* https://www.dailyhuman.com/post/mindful-ai#:~:text=Mindful%20AI%20refers%20to%20the,%2C%20compassion%2C%20and%20ethical%20judgement.

- *The Future of AI: What 2024 Holds for Responsible and ...* https://thomasramsoy.com/index.php/2024/01/15/the-future-of-ai-what-2024-holds-for-responsible-and-ethical-ai/

- *Artificial Intelligence and Quantum Computing - S&P Global* https://www.spglobal.com/en/research-insights/special-reports/artificial-intelligence-and-quantum-computing-the-fundamentals#:~:text=Quantum%20computing's%20combination%20with%20artificial,both%20areas%20have%20been%20remarkable.

- *Artificial Intelligence: Reshaping the Job Market in 2024 ...* https://www.linkedin.com/pulse/artificial-intelligence-reshaping-job-market-2024-beyond-chiancone-kmkdc

- *What Is Human-Centered AI (HCAI)? — updated 2024 | IxDF* https://www.interaction-design.org/literature/topics/human-centered-ai#:~:text=HCAI%20systems%20adapt%20and%20learn,understanding%20of%20human%2DAI%20interaction.

- *Ethical concerns mount as AI takes bigger decision-making ...* https://news.harvard.edu/gazette/story/2020/10/ethical-concerns-mount-as-ai-takes-bigger-decision-making-role/

- *How AI Tools Both Help and Hinder Equity* https://www.insidehighered.com/news/tech-innovation/artificial-intelligence/2023/06/05/how-ai-tools-both-help-and-hinder-equity

- *United Nations System White Paper on AI Governance* https://unsceb.org/united-nations-system-white-paper-ai-governance

- *50 AI Terms Every Beginner Should Know | TELUS Digital* https://www.telusdigital.com/insights/ai-data/article/50-beginner-ai-terms-you-should-know

- *Integrating Mindfulness in AI: A New Frontier for Ethical ...* https://www.dailyhuman.com/post/mindful-ai#:~:text=Mindful%20AI%20refers%20to%20the,%2C%20compassion%2C%20and%20ethical%20judgement.

- *100+ Machine Learning Projects with Source Code [2024]* https://www.geeksforgeeks.org/machine-learning-projects/

- *Boost Your Productivity with Generative AI* https://hbr.org/2023/06/boost-your-productivity-with-generative-ai
- *Decoding AI: A Simplified Glossary* https://www.servicetarget.com/blog/ai-glossary
- *5 AI Ethics Concerns the Experts Are Debating* https://iac.gatech.edu/featured-news/2023/08/ai-ethics
- *AI Adoption by Industry: Top Use Cases Uncovered* https://indatalabs.com/blog/ai-adoption-by-industry
- *Building trust in AI requires a strategic approach* https://www.ibm.com/resources/guides/predict/trustworthy-ai/build-trust/
- *AI-enabled adaptive learning systems: A systematic ...* https://www.sciencedirect.com/science/article/pii/S2666920X21000114
- *Virtual Reality in Education: Benefits, Uses & Examples* https://builtin.com/articles/virtual-reality-in-education
- *Interview with Aylin Caliskan: AI, bias, and ethics - AIhub* https://aihub.org/2023/10/18/interview-with-aylin-caliskan-ai-ethics/
- *How to build an AI community* https://www.linkedin.com/pulse/how-build-ai-community-christophe-zoghbi

About the Author – Dr. Cedric B. Howard

(Author and 3CAT Convener)

Dr. Cedric B. Howard has nearly three decades of experience in higher education and is widely recognized as a pivotal figure in the field. His unwavering dedication and significant contributions have made a lasting impact, earning him the respect and admiration of colleagues and students. In addition to his academic pursuits, Dr. Howard has effectively managed projects across diverse industries, demonstrating his versatility and leadership in both academic and professional realms.

During the COVID-19 pandemic, Dr. Howard convened a cohort of scholar-practitioners and context experts to collaborate on this book (3CAT), drawing upon their collective expertise to address the pressing challenges of our time.

About 3CAT

3CAT is a collective of professionals collaborating across various disciplines to offer innovative and practical solutions for individuals seeking to comprehend the effects of artificial intelligence (AI). Our mission is to disseminate education and information that enhance lives and provide valuable insights into the evolving technological landscape. We believe knowledge is a powerful tool, but its true potential is realized only through practical application.

At 3CAT, we recognize the uniqueness of every individual, which is why we provide diverse training and guidance materials tailored to accommodate various learning preferences and needs. Our publications cover a wide range of essential topics aimed at deepening understanding and knowledge in key areas of interest.

Each publication is the result of collaborative research, expert topic development, and a comprehensive manuscript creation process. We oversee the entire publication journey to ensure the highest quality work, bringing the best solutions to those seeking to navigate the complexities of AI and beyond.

www.ingramcontent.com/pod-product-compliance
Lightning Source LLC
LaVergne TN
LVHW022109200926
848481LV00003B/1123